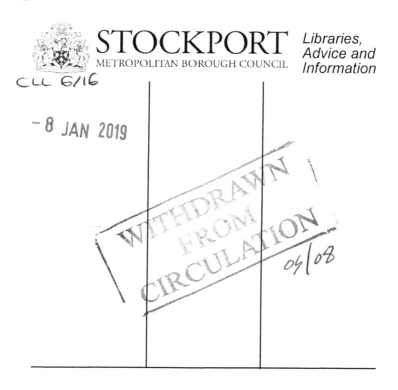

Trembling on the Edge of Eternity

Father Augustine Hoey obl. OSB: A Biographical Memoir

The Hundredth Birthday Edition

Antony Pinchin & Graeme Jolly obl. OSB

© Antony Pinchin & Graeme Jolly

The authors have asserted their rights, under the Copyright, Designs and Patents Act, 1988, to be identified as the authors of this work.

British Library Cataloguing in Publication data

A catalogue record for this book is available from the British Library

ISBN 978-0-907077-69-5

First published in 2015
by St Michael's Abbey Press,
Farnborough Abbey,
Farnborough, Hampshire GU14 7NQ

Second "Hundredth Birthday" Edition:
© St Michael's Abbey Press 2016

www.farnboroughabbey.org
www.theabbeyshop.com

St Michael's Abbey Press is a division of
St Michael's Abbey Press Ltd (reg. no. 326241)

Printed and bound in the Republic of Slovakia

Contents

Acknowledgements

This volume would have been impossible to compile without the patient cooperation of its subject. Fr Augustine Hoey has opened his memory and his emotions to us in a very candid fashion. Despite the fact that at the outset he could not understand why anyone would be interested in reading about his life, during interviews with him over a period lasting more than two years, Fr Augustine has willingly shared the material of his life over the last century. We have been very fortunate that at key moments in his adult life he recorded, in short memoranda, his thoughts and feelings. These documents have been invaluable, representing as they do a contemporary account of events which occurred, in many cases, a long time ago.

In large part this book is a sketch in his own words of the things that have happened to him and the things that matter to him alongside accounts from a range of eye witnesses to this extraordinary life.

It was Stephen Groves, a former student at Mirfield and friend of Fr Augustine who first suggested this project. A member of Augustine's family, his niece Pippa Luckraft, has shared a vast array of family photographs and filled in gaps of family history and we are thankful for all that she has done to assist us.

As half of Fr Augustine's life so far was spent in the Community of the Resurrection we are greatly indebted to the Superior and the Community for their cooperation. In particular Brother Steven Haws CR has worked tirelessly to uncover archive material. Fr Antony Grant CR and Fr Eric Simmons CR as well as their confreres, Brother Roy France CR, Fr Crispin Harrison CR and the late Fr Dominic Whitnall CR were extremely generous in helping us account for Fr Augustine's long association with the community in many different guises.

It was necessary in completing this project to consult a number of other archives and we happily acknowledge the assistance of Stephen Porter (Charterhouse), Dr Nicholas Davidson (St Edmund Hall, Oxford) and

Jacquie Gunn (Ripon College Cuddesdon); Anthony Keogh; and Sr Jo Chambers, SNDdeN.

What has moved us most is the impact that Fr Augustine has had on those with whom he comes into contact and many people have shared their personal reminiscences with us. We are immensely grateful to them all, especially: Vanessa Jones; Jillian Bell-Scott; Jean Hall; Susan and Richard Adams; Sarah Goad; Baron Williams of Oystermouth (former Archbishop of Canterbury, the Most Revd Rowan Williams); Revd Steven Lambert; Jacqueline, Countess de Brosses; Revd Canon Michael Whitehead; Most Revd George Stack, Archbishop of Cardiff; Bernard Grill; Revd Dr Malcolm Johnson; Revd William Nichol; Revd Graham Weir; Dylan Parry; Revd Kevin Robinson; Revd Christopher Jackson; Revd Carl Davies; Revd Mark McIntyre.

Finally we thank the Right Revd Abbot Cuthbert Brogan OSB and St Michael's Abbey Press for advice and encouragement and readily accepting this book for publication.

Antony Pinchin
Graeme Jolly obl. OSB
Feast of Corpus Christi, 2015

Foreword

by the Right Reverend and the Right Honourable
the Lord Williams of Oystermouth

Augustine Hoey was already a legendary figure when I first began work at the College of the Resurrection in the 1970's. Many people had been surprised by his withdrawal from the parish missions in which he had made such an extraordinary name to become a solitary, originally in a council flat in Manchester — where I vividly remember visiting him. A little later, he transferred with a couple of other CR brothers to Sunderland, and I made a memorable pre-ordination retreat there. It was clear that the intensity of the contemplative life, lived in the middle of conditions of real privation, was the natural fruit of all those years of sharing the faith so generously and imaginatively. If it is true that the best sermons are the ones you preach to yourself, Augustine's selfless sharing of the gospel will have more and more opened up that fundamental hunger and emptiness of spirit that draws people deeper into contemplation — so the solitary calling shouldn't surprise us after all. He has been a great gift of God to me throughout my ministry, and I am so pleased that his life is at last being celebrated in a book like this.

Rowan Williams

Foreword

by the Most Reverend George Stack,
Archbishop of Cardiff

I first met Fr Augustine Hoey as he prepared for ordination to the Catholic priesthood at Westminster Cathedral in the mid 1990's. As Administrator of the Cathedral during those years, I worked closely with Cardinal Basil Hume as he charted a way forward for those Anglican clergy and laity who wished to be received into Full Communion with the Catholic Church. The large congregation which attended the ordination of Fr Hoey, and its diversity, were a testament to his profound influence on the spiritual journey of so many during his life and ministry as an Anglican.

One lovely moment remains with me of the scene in the sacristy after the ceremony. Fr Hoey looked totally "surprised by joy" at the warmth and affection shown by his new colleagues in the Diocese of Westminster. It was through the sensitivity and imagination of Cardinal Hume that Fr Hoey has been able to continue his personal religious discipline as a Benedictine Oblate and serve the Church as a Catholic priest — recognised everywhere by his Benedictine habit and his 'cappello Romano'. His faith, trust and courage in making this decision have made Fr Hoey an inspiration to others. So too have his gifts of humility, energy and joy as he continues to preach and teach, to guide and counsel and celebrate the sacraments. I join with so many others in gratitude for his example and am delighted that, through this book, the life, work and character of this remarkable man will be made even more widely known.

+ *George Stack*

chapter 1

Childhood in Leeds

IN THE CHURCH OF THE HOLY SPIRIT, Beeston, Leeds I had, as a child of nine or ten, what can only be described as an intense spiritual experience, which marks the beginning of my thirst for God. It was at a Sung Eucharist and, as I was not a regular worshipper and had received little instruction about the 'catholic way' to God, I was only dimly aware of what the Eucharist was all about. I remember it was a children's mass, at a nave altar which was pulled temporarily into position for the service. After the priest had recited the words of institution, he prostrated himself in silent adoration before the altar for about five minutes. This was the custom in many Tractarian churches in order to emphasise the Real Presence of Christ in the Sacrament. I knew nothing about the latter teaching, but at that moment I was suddenly 'caught up'. I seemed to be surrounded by thousands of 'living presences' who were all intent on adoration. It was marvellous and I wanted to stay.

Kenneth Thomas Hoey was born on 22 December, 1915, into a professional family. He lived in Cranbrook Avenue, Beeston, a comfortable suburb of Leeds. He was prone to pneumonia as a child and was not expected to live. Writing later in life, in a reflection on times when he 'should have died', Hoey shares an early memory:

About three years of age I had severe pneumonia (this was the third time since birth). I have a clear memory of people standing round the bed as I seemed to come out of myself and hover above them, watching them and seeing myself lying there. Then I saw my mother bending lower and lower over me, willing me not to die; gradually she pulled me back into my body. The crisis was over. I did not regret the return, but I often wonder how far it has been responsible for my very complicated relationship with her, varying between total blind adulation and extreme criticism and rejection. This is a very strong memory — I don't know but I think I must have died.

The risk of bronchitis meant that Kenneth's life had many restrictions. The question came up of how and where to go to school, given the need to avoid going out in the cold air. It was thought best that he not be allowed out until noon each day.

Augustine Hoey with his sister, Patricia

In 1920 Kenneth began at Cockburn's School, a pioneer co-educational establishment in Leeds. His attendance was *on and off, doing Prep when not allowed to go to school.* This pattern left great gaps in his education and Hoey claims, to this day, to know *nothing about Geography.*

His father, Albert Edward Hoey, was an industrialist, born in Heckmondwike, with two factories employing hundreds in the manufacture of footwear including boots for the Armed Forces. Albert was well connected and had a close circle of business friends. His mother, Winifred, nee Gath, born in Leeds, did not have to work and ran the house. A fellow member of the Community of the Resurrection in later life, Br Roy France CR, who knew her, described her as 'a determined Yorkshire woman'. Kenneth was eight years old when his sister Patricia was born and they were always close as children and, later, as adults.

Both parents had been brought up as devout Anglicans, his mother having learned the Christian Faith at Leeds Parish Church. After their marriage both had lapsed to an extent. They had no objection to their son going to church on Sunday mornings if he was well enough and the weather was alright. Kenneth was taught to say his prayers and read from Arthur Lee's 'Bible stories for children' in which he recalls that *each story had a marvellous picture which, when reading in Church, still comes before my eyes.*

On big occasions, the family would go to Leeds Parish Church and sit in a pew in the gallery facing the pulpit. *My memory is that I could not see over the top. I can picture faces but not think of details. There was a great deal of music.*

Albert Edward Hoey, father

Kenneth fell easily into the habit of attending Leeds Parish Church, alone when not accompanying the family, but found the elaborate singing of Mattins tedious and not really holding any meaning for him. His religious instincts emerged in other ways, this incident after the experience of Beeston being one:

Hoey's mother, Winifred

Nothing used to give me more delight, in common with many other children, than to be given a sixpence to spend in Woolworths, for in those days no article in the store was beyond that price! It was the only store, too, where one could wander round to one's heart's content, even without a sixpence, to gaze at the multitude of goods and decide what to buy next, when in funds. It was on one of these looking around days that I suddenly saw some crucifixes. I immediately thought, 'I must have one of those.'

I don't know why I was so sure, because my religion was not yet 'meat and drink' to me. I realised too, in some strange way, that there might be some opposition to the idea at home. There was. "Crucifixes are only for Catholics," said my mother, "I don't know where you get such ideas from."

However, I persisted and in due time was able to buy one. The only stipulation was that I must keep it in my bedroom. I hung it by my bed with great satisfaction, little realising that it was a sign, unconscious as yet, of the tremendous religious ferment shortly to boil up within me. I used to look at it — not with formal prayer — but thinking how marvellous it must be to love as much as that.

His mother was somewhat critical of the Church of the Holy Spirit, Beeston, the location of his first spiritual experience "because of its Anglo-Catholic 'goings on'". Soon, from her point of view, worse was to come, when Kenneth was twelve.

I had a friend called Reginald. One Sunday morning we decided we would go to Church. It was Trinity Sunday and when I look back, this was a turning-point. We set out for Leeds Parish Church. We got as far as a church called Christ Church in Meadow Lane and when we looked up at the clock in the tower we realised we would be too late if we went on. We went into the church, which was very full, and there a full High Mass was just beginning. I shall never forget it. It somehow crystallised my 'experience' of the Eucharist in the Church of the Holy Spirit. It came back to me with greater depth of meaning and I realised I was at the beginning of a way from which there was no turning back. I was both fascinated and overwhelmed. When we got back, I told my

Christ Church, Meadow Lane, Leeds
(now demolished)

parents and they were very cross, saying to me, "It's a high church place; you have no business going in there."

The priest, Fr Philip Strong, took their names and addresses. Next day he arrived at the door to visit and for Kenneth there began the whole process of 'becoming an Anglo-Catholic', somewhat to his parents' bemusement. Reginald, on the other hand, was forbidden to return to Christ Church.

At the age of thirteen, Kenneth decided he wanted to be Confirmed. His parents came to his Confirmation and, overcoming their reticence about its 'goings-on', they continued to attend Christ Church, returning to the regular reception of Holy Communion from then on. Christ Church, Meadow Lane was a slum parish. Hoey's mother did charity work there supporting the 'Boots for the Bairns' campaign, which provided for children who had no shoes.

Attendance at school had become more regular and Hoey's teenage life went on more or less as normal albeit with its moments of risk and even danger.

I was 14 years old and had gone with a friend and his family on holiday to Filey. The cliffs there on the way to the Brigg are very steep. In one place there is a memorial tablet at the base of the cliffs to a boy who fell into the sea while climbing and was drowned. Nothing daunted, I was sure I could climb the cliffs! At first it seemed easy and there were many tufts of grass to which I could cling. Soon it became more difficult and as I looked down I saw I was now above the sea (I could not then swim) and not the beach. However, I was determined to go on and slowly, with many slips and slides, I moved on until the moment when I was stuck. I felt petrified. I looked up. The top of the cliff seemed far away and was hanging over me. I looked down and saw I was just above the memorial tablet against which the waves were beating and throwing up clouds of spray. I was stiff with fear and terrified to move lest I rolled into the sea. I looked up again and managed to scramble up about a foot to a tuft of grass which began to give way as I clutched it, and then held. Suddenly I felt myself being pushed upwards almost flat against the cliff side with the soil and the stones falling away beneath my feet until I lay gasping and terrified on the grassy cliff top. I have always believed it was my guardian angel who rescued me from certain death. Only Divine intervention could have carried me up the overhanging cliff side.

The recollection of this experience still evokes within me the same terror and anxiety I had there and it is difficult to face. Is it because the whole incident was due to disobedience?

Hoey's sister Patricia had by now gone to school with the sisters at Whitby and Kenneth was *fascinated by nuns and pestered her with questions.*

At school, Hoey showed both academic and leadership potential. He was prepared for, and passed, the entrance exam for Oxford. He also became Head Boy. His Headmaster, Mr Norden (who worshipped at Christ Church, Meadow Lane), commented in a reference for St Edmund Hall, Oxford in January, 1935, on his "exceedingly good influence" at the school: "He has thrown himself whole-heartedly into all our activities, even into those for which he has little natural aptitude".

Reflecting many years later on the most significant moment of his childhood, his experience at

Members of Kenneth's Father's family. Clockwise from top left: Uncle George, Aunt Elizabeth, Martha and Thomas (the parents), Aunts Jane, Lillian and Mary.

Holy Spirit, Beeston, Hoey wrote this in 1973:

Church of the Holy Spirit, Beeston (now closed)

> *As with all such experiences of the reality of God, it can never be put into words or music. It seemed as if I was 'up there' and looking down at the rows of children kneeling before their chairs. I wasn't afraid but only glad and wanting it to go on for ever. Gradually the 'vision' faded and I was kneeling in my place watching the people receiving Holy Communion.*
>
> *I used the word 'vision' because I was dimly aware of visual forms as well as great light and of a sound in my ears which was unlike ordinary music and yet wholly absorbing and ecstatic. The experience has never left me, nor been repeated in exactly the same way, but it has lain at the heart of all my subsequent search for God.*
>
> *It also marked the beginning of a great devotion to the Blessed Sacrament — not consciously at the time, but subsequently after I had received instruction in the faith and met 'Reservation', I realised the implications of the context of my vision. I know — whichever way theological argument may ebb and flow — that the Risen, Ascended Christ is present in the Blessed Sacrament both in the Eucharist and in Reservation. This conviction may have its origin in a subjective experience as a child, but it is something I shall never be able to deny.*

chapter 2
Oxford

WHILE WAITING TO GO UP to Oxford, Kenneth Hoey suffered a crisis in the form of a bout of so-called 'Roman Fever'. This was an experience in the lives of many Anglo-Catholics, most clearly documented in the life of Blessed John Henry Newman. Newman decided over a period of time that he no longer had confidence in the catholic authenticity of the Church of England. After a period of uncertainty he finally concluded "the spell is broken" and was received into the Catholic Church by the Passionist priest, Blessed Dominic Barberi.

'Roman Fever' resembles a disease which can lie dormant for years, flaring up occasionally before finally claiming its host. The greater the emphasis, that for example a catholic-minded Anglican places on historic continuity and solidity of catholic doctrine, the more he or she is likely to look 'over the fence' to the Roman Catholic Church at an intellectual level. Yet at the level of aesthetics in worship, community spirit or family ties, a certain inertia may hold the person affected back from actually making a definitive move.

Hoey's summary of this period is brief: *I used to enjoy going into St Anne's (Catholic) Cathedral, Leeds to observe and pray. I realised I needed to decide. I just made a decision to stay where I was.*

Underlying this was a sense of vocation to the priesthood which he had felt since his Confirmation at the age of 13, yet spoke little of. A sense of vocation to a particular Anglican ministry can only intensify the poignancy of any 'Roman Crisis'.

In October 1935 Hoey went up to Oxford to read Modern History, matriculating at St Edmund Hall. As with many undergraduates, his interest in the subject of his degree was not the most significant aspect of his time at Oxford — he took a third class degree. He later reflected on his time at Oxford in this way: *I am not a scholar. I was not really interested in history and wished that I had read Theology — I don't really know much theology at all.* Theatre and spirituality played a more significant role in his life. A member of the College Dramatic Society he *had the odd flirtation with the idea of the stage.* His father had been in Gilbert and Sullivan productions and there were performances at home, including a scaled-down 'Iolanthe'.

Kenneth experienced a hesitation in vocation in his second year. He recalls an all-male 'Richard II' directed by John Gielgud and Vivienne Lee at the Oxford University Dramatic Society production in 1936, and playing Bolingbroke.

Vivienne Lee was at the start of her career and Hoey later recalled that *she had porcelain beauty and only conversation about sex and men.* This episode is the first in which we see the dapper Hoey brushing against high society. Connections were established, one fruit of which was that in the years to come his ordination stole would be designed by Norman Hartnell (though he no longer has it).

The Oxford Anglican 'divine' J. N. D Kelly, author of seminal works such as 'Early Christian Doctrines', even before completing his year as a deacon in a parish, was invited to return to Oxford as Chaplain and tutor in theology and philosophy at St Edmund Hall by the then principal, A.B. Emden. In 1937, Kelly was made Vice-Principal and later Principal.

J.N.D. Kelly as Principal of St Edmund Hall in later life

Despite the theatrical interlude, the spiritual life claimed pride of place during Hoey's undergraduate years, creating a continuity between term-time and vacation.

> On the first Sunday I went to Mass in College. Only three colleges had a daily Mass, Keble, St Edmund and Christ Church. I went to the 8 a.m. in College and then to the Cowley Fathers (the Anglican religious community known as The Society of Saint John the Evangelist). I suppose they were at the peak of their success. They were terribly austere — Saint John's Church, Cowley, was packed to the doors and the congregation was divided into male and female.

Anglo-Catholicism in the 1930s, and to some extent in modern times, covered a spectrum from great devotion to the Book of Common Prayer and classical Anglicanism on the one hand to outright Romanism with the borrowing of Catholic ritual and liturgical dress on the other.

On the second Sunday I went to Pusey House which was under Fr Frederick Hood, a great producer of vocations. Only men attended. On weekdays the English Missal (a translation into Cranmer's English of the Tridentine Missal) was used. I served at Pusey House.

Hoey normally alternated between Pusey House (where he served as thurifer) and St John's, Cowley. He *liked the worship at Pusey*, but as thoughts of becoming a religious developed he also felt the Cowley Fathers offered a spiritual home, and it was there that he found a Confessor.

In the next room at St Edmund Hall lived Colin Stephenson, a year senior to Kenneth. They became great friends and Stephenson took Hoey on his first visit to the Anglican Benedictine monks at Nashdom Abbey in Buckinghamshire (his cousin was a monk there). In due course Stephenson, who later became well known as the Administrator at the Anglican Shrine of Our Lady of Walsingham, left Oxford for Chichester Theological College, though the two men remained friends until Stephenson's death.

During my late teens and years at Oxford, the Mass and the Blessed Sacrament began to claim me more and more. I went to Mass daily and have done ever since when it is physically possible. I would often feel quite overwhelmed by a sense of the 'beyond' during the Eucharistic Prayer and a growing grief that the 'world' did not seem able to 'see' that Christ is in our midst. Once in the Cowley Fathers' church during the Sunday High Mass, I had a vivid awareness of Christ crucified, with arms stretched out on the Cross to touch the very ends of the earth. I can still see it now.

I seemed more and more compelled to visit the Blessed Sacrament. Sometimes at home, in the middle of studying, I would put down my books and walk rapidly over a mile to the nearest church where the Sacrament was reserved. When I arrived there, hot and breathless, I could frequently neither pray nor think; it was enough to be there and the lower part of my mind seemed rooted in wordless awe while at the same time the surface of my mind was often crowded with distraction.

I remember staying with a college friend at his home in Burgess Hill. The church was opposite and the Sacrament was reserved. I was sleeping in another house just up the road and I would, during the day, frequently make the excuse of going there to get something, but instead I would slip into the church to kneel by the aumbry.

I could continue this account of the Mass and the Blessed Sacrament taking possession of my life ad nauseam. It has never faltered and is now stronger than ever — nor does it obliterate the great truths of Christ being also present in the Baptised soul, in the Word of the New Testament and in His Church. In fact all become indefinably one.

There are two other episodes belonging to Kenneth Hoey's student days which were moments of no return.

One Sunday evening while walking in Oxford with a friend (JNDK) [J. N. D. Kelly, the College Chaplain] *and passing Fairacres Road, he said, "Have you ever been in the Chapel of the Fairacres sisters?" "No," I replied, "I have never heard of them." We went through a little gate in Fairacres Road, which I think I could have passed a hundred times without noticing. Certainly it had 'Convent of the Incarnation' written on it, but the gate was narrow and wedged in the middle of a row of dreary suburban houses. A short drive led to the chapel door and on going inside I found myself in the south transept of the chapel, a grille cutting us off from the rest of the chapel. It was the first time I had stood on the threshold of an enclosed order. A nun was kneeling motionless before the Blessed Sacrament; a clock chimed somewhere and another nun came in to replace her. So the perpetual intercession was maintained.*

I was overcome by the numinousness of the chapel, by the sense of great stirring and activity at the love which was being so lavishly poured out by the sisters on behalf of mankind. I left in a daze. I didn't really want to go on talking to my friend, because I was so overwhelmed by the experience. I returned as soon as I could and through the years, whenever I have been in Oxford, it has acted like a magnet. I realised at the time, in a dim kind of way, I was being drawn to the kind of life lived there, but I was terrified to face it, because the renunciation seemed too great and would be such a terrible shock to my parents, who had made so many sacrifices for me.

I had already decided I should be a priest and this vocation had grown simultaneously with my preparation for the Sacraments. This had caused some bewilderment for my parents, but they had accepted it and I was up at Oxford 'on them' without any grants at all. What I had not yet told them was my inner drawing to the religious life, which was gradually asserting itself.

A second episode belonging to Oxford days was perhaps of even greater significance. Hoey made his first visit to Walsingham in 1937, six years after the reconstruction of the Holy House. He travelled there with Kelly. The medieval shrine had been constructed following the vision of Our Lady by Richeldis de Faverches in 1061. The Shrine was brought back to life, after the destruction of the Protestant Reformation and centuries of neglect, by the Anglican priest Fr Alfred Hope-Patten. The Holy House and the Church which rose to contain it, has played a central role in Hoey's life ever since this first visit. It is the place where his vocation would lead him for the closing years of his life. Further, it was the

The Holy House, Walsingham, 1931

location where his awareness of a call to a life of intercession began — of prayer for others and for the world.

We had gone on a journey of 'curiosity' to Walsingham and I at that time was prepared to be critical of everything I had heard about the [Anglican] Shrine and its activities. I was a bit taken aback on first entering the Holy House and thought its sense of mystery deliberately contrived — rather like a theatre set. We stayed overnight and before leaving I went again to the Holy House. I knelt and shut my eyes to all the 'props' and began to pray for others; I was drawn deeper and deeper into intercession in a way I had never experienced before. Time passed, I was unaware of it; I had to stay. Finally, I wrenched myself away, knowing JNDK must be getting impatient. He was. I had been praying

11

for an hour! My desire for a life directed to intercession stems from this moment. It had fallen on me like a bolt from the blue in the Holy House, perhaps because that is a place where so much 'beseeching' for stricken humanity is linked with the prayer of Mary. So Walsingham has become for me a very special place. I have since visited many of the Shrines of Christendom, but nowhere which repeatedly has given me the feeling of time and eternity rolling into one and awakening in me the necessity to intercede.

Reflecting later, Hoey refers to the particular way in which Our Lady invited him to share in her maternal role.

The Anglican Holy House had just been built; the Shrine Church was built around it later. As I stood before Our Lady's image I became transfixed; I saw no vision nor heard any audible voice; the statue became a living person... sitting on her throne... just as alive as I was. The words welled up within me, "She is mothering the world." I realised I was to share in her 'mothering' and my vocation was to spend my life giving priority to intercession. I have always felt this and tried to work to this end even though at times my days have been overloaded with other religious activities, such as missions. Because of this the Holy House will always be for me a place trembling on the edge of Eternity.

The Anglican Shrine in 1931

Hoey took his BA in Modern History in 1938 (MA 1944). He moved to Pusey House in Michaelmas Term 1938 and lived there for a term while waiting to enter Cuddesdon in January 1939.

The Anglican Theological College at Cuddesdon, situated in a village outside Oxford, was at the time based on a quasi-monastic model. Students attended a fourfold office — Morning and Evening Prayer, Mid-day Prayer and Night Prayer. No speaking was permitted in the village, with Greater and Lesser silences strictly observed within the college. Students were only allowed to go into Oxford on Saturdays from 1 to 6 p.m. The Principal, Eric Graham, later a Bishop in the Scottish Episcopal Church, was married with six children but he and his wife lived like religious — the youngest child was born while her father celebrated the Eucharist in Chapel. Hoey recalls that living conditions, even by comparison with pre-war Oxford life were "appalling" with inadequate heating and one bath to serve seven rooms.

Hoey continued to dress elegantly — he had 30 suits to choose from, *made by a tailor out of friendship*, and wore a bow tie.

In his second year, priests arrived to pick curates, among them Fr Ralph Bell CR, a Mirfield Father who was Vicar of the Parish of Saint Mary of Eton, Hackney Wick in the East End of London. The Principal, aware of Hoey's interest in the religious life, proposed him to Fr Bell and the move was agreed.

chapter 3

St Mary of Eton

KENNETH THOMAS HOEY was ordained Deacon at St Paul's Cathedral by Geoffrey Fisher, in the first Ordination he carried out as Bishop of London, on Trinity Sunday, 18th May, 1940. He describes this as *a spiritual moment, splendid, with full choir.* The ordination retreat had taken place at Fulham Palace (the then residence of the Bishop of London) during the week beforehand. The ordinands slept in large dormitories, originally meant for servants, up in the roof. *In a study big enough for us all to stand round — thirty to forty people, Geoffrey Fisher interviewed each one of us individually — he told me, "The East End will be very good for you." I recall him standing with his back to the fire and saying, "Pacifists, step forward! Go next door. I'll deal with you later." I quite liked him — he always remembered you. Dinner was quite an occasion with Mrs Fisher in elegant skirts or a full dinner dress. On the eve of ordination Fisher said, "Breakfast tomorrow will be as usual. Some of you may feel scrupulous and eat simply; others, unwisely, will go fasting."*

An Anglican mission financed by Eton College was originally founded in Malford Street, London E9, above an undertaker's shop. In 1884 an iron church was erected, and in 1892 a new church was built to the designs of E.F. Bodley, with funds provided by Eton College. In 1893 the mission became a parish, comprising the parishes of Saint Augustine Hackney Wick and Saint Barnabas Homerton. The church was enlarged and a tower added in 1911-1912. It is now surrounded by elevated motorways.

At the start of the Second World War, the serving Vicar of St Mary of Eton had joined the Army. Eton College asked the Community of the Resurrection (CR) based in Mirfield, West Yorkshire, if they would staff the parish and they sent Fr Ralph Bell, CR. The CR house in London had been bombed, so the London fathers lived in the Hackney Wick Clergy House and in this way Deacon Hoey came to know CR. The Religious Life had constantly been at the back of his mind — *it was what I wanted* — but with the start of parish work Hoey *was relieved at leaving it all behind.*

St Mary's was BCP (Book of Common Prayer) plus. Our Lady did not dominate but Confessions were heard. There was therefore a catholic tradition but the parish was by no means leaning towards Rome in its celebration of the liturgy.

Hoey's ordination to the Anglican Priesthood, took place on Trinity Sunday, 7th June 1941, in the Crypt of St Paul's Cathedral and was a much simpler

St Mary of Eton, Hackney Wick – a photograph taken for the builders of the Bodley Church

affair than his ordination to the Diaconate. The examination before his priesting was carried out among debris from an attack during the Blitz. His Anglican First Mass was celebrated on the Thursday following, 11th June. Holy Communion was given from the tabernacle at 5.00 a.m., and then Fr Kenneth Hoey celebrated High Mass of Corpus Christi at 5.30 a.m.

While this was a great moment, it does not seem to have been a turning point in Hoey's spiritual life. His attendance at daily mass stretched back through Oxford days and has continued throughout his life, but he says little about celebrating the Eucharist as a priest and recalls few details of the liturgy at St Mary's. In his spiritual journey, a more memorable event was to follow.

> *For Corpus Christi 1941 I took some parishioners to Burnham Abbey (home of the community of nuns known as the Society of the Precious Blood) for the Procession. I had only visited the Abbey once before to have lunch with the Warden, Fr Biggart CR, who resided there for the duration of the war. I felt from the first a strong attraction to all that SPB stood for in the life of the Church. At the end of the Procession, one of the nuns came and said, "Mother Foundress (Mother Millicent of the Will of God) would like to speak to you."*

In one of two accounts of the event, Hoey continues:

> *I was taken to the parlour. I felt a bit nervous about this for I knew nothing about her and still don't know to this day what prompted her to want to see me. I felt rather 'singled out' for the Abbey Grounds were*

full of guests, whom I felt sure would have loved to take my place. I remember being rather tongue-tied and slightly overawed by Mother Millicent as she sat on the other side of the grille and there seemed to cling around her a great sense of perfect stillness. She spoke of the religious life (and I wondered how she knew because it was still a secret locked in my own heart) and also of the Passion of Christ.

In another account he recalls other details:

MM "What parish are you from? I think I should tell you that you should dedicate your life to prayer. I was observing you in the Procession."
AH "I am to test my vocation to the religious life."
MM "That will keep you safe."
I left her thinking, 'I shall have to do something about it soon'. But in fact I dallied a further three years. Her dissertation on the Passion struck a chord for I had long felt specially drawn to Gethsemane and always kept vigil all night on Maundy Thursday.

Hoey's earliest contacts with religious communities in the Church of England had centred on the Cowley Fathers in Oxford but after the visit to Mother Millicent his interest in the religious life shifted emphasis from Cowley to Mirfield. He felt CR to be *more human* and recalls that on retreat with the Cowley Fathers he had felt *weighed down by austerity.*

These spiritual events took place against the background of the life of an Anglo-Catholic East-End parish in the extraor-dinary circumstances of the Second World War. Peace-time life in such parishes followed a disciplined, devoted and energetic schedule, with the daily celebration of Morning and Evening Prayer

With Fr James Woodrow CR in parish days

17

and of the Eucharist in Church, The routine would include Sunday School, regular meetings of children's and adult organisations and visiting every home in the geographical parish.

Everyone in the parish was knocked up once per month; it was a very compact area. We were always out. There was no hostility. The children were at Sunday school, back already from evacuation. There were never fewer than fifteen people at Evensong, held during the blackout by torchlight. There were three priests and three 'Eton ladies'. *Fr Ralph said, 'we mustn't all be killed at once' so we slept in different places — an Anderson shelter in the garden, the Church and the Hall.* During the Blitz Hoey recalls a strange mixture of *raids, spending time in shelters and visiting elderly bed-ridden spinsters. There were bombs most nights but we didn't think about death.* A peculiarity was that the local fish and chip shop acquired a new importance since restaurants and cafés were not rationed. *Contact with Roman Catholics was just polite. We didn't give RCs a great deal of thought. They had a church, school and nuns.* Fr Hoey taught in a local school and was greeted by a Roman Catholic child with the accusation, "Sister says you're not real."

An almost legendary event occurred early on the evening of Thursday 27th July, 1944. It made the front page of the Daily Express the next day. Hoey described the event in notes written later.

> *I was an assistant priest in the parish of St Mary of Eton, Hackney Wick all through the war and lived through the air raids and the devastating bombing. One evening at around 5 p.m., during the time of the V1 flying bomb attacks. I was sitting in my room in the Clergy House giving an instruction for Confirmation when the familiar buzz of a flying bomb was heard and the air raid sirens began to wail. I said to the nurse I was instructing, "Do you want to take shelter?" We agreed not, because the situation was so familiar. I heard the bomb switch off its buzz, which was the sign it was coming down. The next thing I remember was being dragged out of a heap of debris and rubble; blood was running down my face. Blast is a strange thing. The nurse was scratched. At 6 p.m. we were in Church saying the Angelus amid the damage. The devastation everywhere was terrific. The Church Tower was cracked from top to bottom; a terrace of houses opposite the church had been blown into the churchyard and formed a vast mountain of debris, half the church roof had disappeared and the windows were blown into splinters.*
>
> *I felt dazed as I was rushed off to the first aid facilities to discover I only had a slight cut on my head which needed four stitches. Otherwise I*

ENEMY STEPS UP BOMB ATTACK

Lancasters hit back at bases

Express Air Reporter

MORE flying bombs came over Southern England, including the London area, after nightfall yesterday, as well as during daylight. The Germans stepped up the attack after a two-day partial lull, but a number of the robots had been destroyed by midnight.

Outside the church

Two were downed one after the other in a South-East Coast area. One crashed in a residential part of a town, causing damage, after being hit by a fighter. The other blew up in mid-air.

A terrific burst of A.A. fire at midnight brought down two more bombs, which exploded in the same district.

The rise and fall in the scale of launchings shows that the enemy is unable to sustain a continuous attack.

It is an indication, too, that the heavy bombing by Allied aircraft of the supply dumps, their feeder lines, and the actual launching sites is having a powerfully limiting effect.

Lancasters and Stirlings again smashed at launching sites in Northern France yesterday.

Like great thunder-claps in a tropical storm, the A.A. barrage roared out along parts of the coast at intervals during the evening.

The gunfire was deafening, and at times fighters, flying low, joined in the battle. At one coast town people saw a Mustang shoot pieces off a bomb as it was coming in. The engine was hit and the robot lost speed before crashing into a field.

Nurse carried on

When a flying bomb crashed within a few yards of a vicarage last night a priest was in his study preparing a nurse for confirmation and he was injured in the head.

She bound up the wound and rushed him to hospital, then cycled to another hospital for night duty. There she was found to be suffering from shock and put to bed.

Family trapped

Twelve people were taken to hospital from one whole housing estate, including one whole family, Mr. and Mrs. Ashby and their four boys, who were trapped in an Anderson shelter.

Search was being made late last night for Miss Morrison, 22, whose mother was reported to have been in one of the houses which received a direct hit. Two persons were so badly hurt that they are not expected to recover.

Resistance chief warns traitors

'You will be tried'

CHERBOURG, Thursday. — Monsieur J. Bocher, resistance movement leader in Cherbourg during the last four years, today warned all French people who have betrayed their country by working for the Germans that they will be tried before the courts.

"The good French, impatient for justice, can be assured that justice will be done," he says.—Express News Service.

Bomb barrage hit U.S. troops

NINTH AIR FORCE H.Q., France, Thursday.—Casualties were caused among front-line American troops by Tuesday's massive American bombing. General Brereton said today.

The air support, which was requested by the Army, was almost exactly what was expected, but he explained that, according to the investigation so far made, some heavy bombers and one group of mediums dropped bombs into the

FRAMED in a church window last night—rescue workers, under a hill of broken masonry.

The priest is hit

He saw his church blasted. Now, with bandaged head, he checks the damage.

DAILY EXPRESS

ONLY 30 MILES TO WARSAW

Tanks are streaming across Vistula

FRANCE: A COMPLETE BREAKTHROUGH

ENEMY STEPS UP BOMB ATTACK

Daily Express Front Page on 28th July 1944

19

was unharmed and was soon back at the scene of devastation. The rubble was being dug through for bodies. All night the digging continued. It was uncanny. The men digging kept stopping and shouting to see if there was any response from the debris. Only silence. Everyone was dead. Why had I been kept alive? I have always thought it was my Guardian Angel who had been instructed that this was not the time for me to journey with the others into the life beyond.

Beyond the routine of parish life and the exigencies of war, there were moments for celebration, festivities and pageants. The Sixtieth Anniversary of the founding of the Mission was celebrated with a Pageant devised by the Assistant Priest and reported in the local paper, with over a hundred children taking part as well as numerous members

Parish pageant

of the Mothers' Union. A crucifer, thurifer and Fr Ralph Bell CR in Cope led a procession representing eighteen saints, each with a banner in front of them, and ending with Saint Mary of Eton 'crowned and seated on a veritable chariot of flowers drawn by a soldier, sailor and airman'. The paper recorded that 'special credit is due to Fr Hoey who organised it'. Another paper commended the celebrations for evoking 'the splendour and romance of the Faith'. Already at St Mary of Eton, Hoey's hallmark combination of devotion and theatre can be seen.

Within the daily round, the sense of a more particular vocation, to the religious life, was ever-present in the young priest's mind. As the Clergy House at St Mary of Eton had become the temporary London home for the Community of the Resurrection, Hoey met many Mirfield fathers and his sense of attraction to the community continued to grow. He applied to join the Novitiate.

In April 1945 the Community elected him and on 24 April 1945 he was admitted to the Novitiate at mass in Mirfield taking the name Augustine.

The Superior of the Community of the Resurrection at that time was Raymond Raynes CR, who had been elected in 1943, and was making

Religious Pageant At Hackney Wick.

ETON MISSION'S PATRONAL WEEK.

The procession and pageant which moved through the streets of Hackney Wick last Sunday afternoon provided something of a climax to the festival week which the parish of St. Mary of Eton has been holding in honour of its patron and its dedication. It was an impressive act of thankfulness and praise for 60 years of vigorous life at the Eton Mission.

The procession was headed by the cross-bearer, the thurifer, and the priest vested in cope (Fr. Bell, C.R., the acting vicar), and there were some eighteen saints represented, each preceded by an appropriate banner. The fitting centre-piece was St. Mary of Eton, crowned and seated on a veritable chariot of flowers, drawn by a soldier, a sailor and an airman, and surrounded by tiny "angels" swathed in white.

But the pageant did more than look back at the past. Ample evidence of the mission's life to-day was afforded by the presence of well over a hundred children from the two Sunday schools, members of the Mothers' Union, and good support from the regular congregation. Mention must also be made of the singing, which was strongly led by the Guild of Christ the King and a volunteer brass band from St. Luke's and the Mayfield Mission. A great deal of hard work had been put in by many willing helpers in the parish to make the pageant a success, and special credit is due to Fr. Hoey, who organised it.

To close the festive day, a large crowd attended solemn even-song, which was sung in the lovely Bodley church. Lady Tallents sang solos from two oratorios, and the preacher was Fr. Aglionby, at one time on the staff of the Eton Mission and now vicar of St. Saviour's, Ealing. The service concluded with a procession round the church, and, as a final act of praise and worship, Psalm 150 was sung.

Old Comrades' D───

Local paper's account of Pageant

many changes, among them moving the community towards a more monastic spirituality and a more 'Roman' style of worship. These developments posed no problems to Hoey, who admired Raynes' practice of monasticism and regarded him as totally given to God. He was reputed to have said about an active religious life, "what does it matter if it kills you?"

Silence was quite strictly observed. There was a general state of 'lesser silence' when talking was only permitted if it was connected with work. In the afternoon there was gardening and time for a walk. A contemporary in the Novitiate of ten men, Fr Dominic Whitnall CR, recalls that during the afternoon when gardening, Augustine wore 'colourful mufti' and was assigned the task by Fr Ralph Bell CR (previously his Acting Vicar at St Mary of Eton) of turning the muck heap; in the house, by contrast, Augustine had a huge rosary stretched across his bed.

Greater Silence was observed from Compline to Terce. Even this regime struck Hoey as less strict than the Cowley Fathers. The daily liturgical routine for the new Novice was:

0600	First Mass
0645	Morning Prayer and Prime
0730	Terce and High Mass (celebrated according to the South African Rite, a liturgical form much closer to the Roman Missal than to the Book of Common Prayer)
1230	Sext
1630	None
1900	Evensong
2030	Compline

The new Novice no doubt faithfully lived the life of the Novitiate, however, just as he had thought longingly about the religious life during his five years in the parish, so in the Community he could never get the parish out of his mind. There was no restriction on correspondence and so much of it came from the parish that he asked them to stop writing. Hoey missed the drama in the streets and the annual pantomime. Seeing the College at Mirfield performing drama brought bleak moments of nostalgia for the East End.

Two thirds of the way through his time in the Novitiate he wrote to the new Vicar in Hackney Wick, Can I come back? and received the answer that he could. Fr Whitnall was "not surprised at his first departure." In September 1946 the Superior informed Chapter that Augustine Hoey had withdrawn from the Novitiate.

chapter 4

Early Mirfield Life

THE RETURN OF FR HOEY to the parish of St Mary of Eton was not a success. His thoughts swiftly returned to the religious life. *I knew within three weeks that I had made a great mistake. The Vicar insisted that I stayed for a year.* He subsequently asked to return to Mirfield and was invited back but had to start at the beginning once more as a Postulant. Records at Mirfield record that on 18th June 1948 Kenneth Hoey was elected to the Novitiate, taking the name of Augustine and that on 22nd June 1948 Augustine Hoey was admitted to the Novitiate at High Mass. From the moment of his second arrival at Mirfield *there was never a doubt again.*

Of the whole experience, Hoey later wrote: *I entered the religious life to structure my life on the work of prayer and to try to make a more total offering of myself to God. I found the wrench from the relationships of parish life, particularly the children, more than I could bear. After a tortured novitiate I went back to the parish. I soon realised it was a wrong decision. The structured prayer of the religious life had laid its hands upon me and I was compelled to return and start again at the beginning. I never had a moment's doubt after the day of my return and all went smoothly along to Profession and nothing since has ever caused me to waver. The return to parish life taught me once and for all that there is no going back to former situations and that what was once 'golden' tarnishes in the attempt to recapture it.*

Weekly instruction was given by the Novice Guardian, Fr Lawrence Wrathal CR, with explanation of the Rule. The Community of the Resurrection based its life on the Rule of Saint Augustine, an inspiration for orders of canons and canonesses in the Catholic Church. There were fifteen or sixteen in the Novitiate this time around. The first year was largely enclosed whilst during the second year, particular abilities were tested — at this time the activities of the community included Children's Missions, Adult Missions and Retreats.

There were also domestic chores to be done. Novices were chaplains to the domestic household including disabled boys who worked for the Fathers. The Novice Master, Fr Lawrence Wrathal CR placed

Augustine in charge of cleaning. Thus began a tradition in which Fr Augustine Hoey was associated with cleaning by his brethren, some of whom, even today, when they hear his name, will draw a finger along a table, shelf or other surface and inspect the finger tip for any dust it might have picked up.

Early days at Mirfield

Novices were permitted £5 for such necessities as toothpaste while any gifts received had to be passed to the Bursar. Two weeks of holiday were allowed, with £10 to fund them. Initially for holidays Augustine went to stay with his parents who then took him away. On one of these holidays the Hoey family visited Lourdes where Hoey registered no 'Roman' impact but was impressed by the nuns he encountered. Later he holidayed with Br Roy France CR, who first met him in 1949 and found him friendly on the personal level. Br Roy recalls that their holidays were always religious — for example to Bruges for ceremonies around the feast of the Precious Blood — and can recall Augustine demonstrating his natural elegance by wearing shorts and a casual top on occasion.

On 23 December 1949 Hoey the Novice was encouraged to make formal application to be elected to full membership of the Community and on 25 July 1950 Augustine made his First Profession (along with Jasper Mduna & Cedma Mack) at High Mass on St James' Day.

A major activity of the community was the running of missions for adults and children and of retreats. Hoey took his place in this work, but it would be fair to say that he evolved his own particular style, drawing on his understanding of the nature of evangelism and on his talent for the dramatic.

Fr Hope Patten, the Vicar of Walsingham, wrote to Mirfield asking for a Mission in 1951 by when Hoey had been professed. He collected together a team. Hoey wrote to say, *I'd like a lifesize crucifix in the aisle — and there it was. AHP was good in things you didn't really associate with him, for example he started up a youth club. He could also be ruthless. If he were a Catholic I think he would be up for canonisation. The spiritual atmosphere during the mission was highly charged. It lasted ten days, finishing on Ascension Day and there was no pilgrimage. There was a daily 6am High Mass with 150-200 villagers.*

Hoey would, at a young age, be renowned as a remarkable exponent of the Mirfield Mission. A Hoey Mission in a parish was an event held in the shared memory of the parish for many years, in some cases even for decades. Apart from individual recollections of such missions, we gain an understanding of how they were conducted from Hoey's book, 'Go Quickly and Tell', which was published in 1959 by The Faith Press. The flyleaf summarises the content:

> Father Augustine Hoey CR during the last decade has pioneered a Mission technique which uses every legitimate modern aid, particularly those of the visual kind... The author displays in his methods a real understanding of the make-up of the ordinary man and woman.

> Fr Hoey has become well known all over the country in the last few years as a Missioner of outstanding gifts.

The table of contents of the book reveals the scope of the Hoey mission philosophy and technique:

I	The Heart of the Matter
II	Interview with the Parish Priest
III	The Preliminary Visit
IV	The 'straight' Mission
V	A Family Mission
VI	Holy Week and Easter
VII	A Bank Holiday Mission at the Seaside
VIII	The 'Follow Up'

The scope of the short book is shown in that, ever-practical, the last page is an illustrated guide to making a flaming torch for outdoor processions, from a used can filled with cotton wool. In the opening page, Hoey writes:

> *Every member of the Church is committed to being an Evangelist. This is a truth which the Holy Spirit has made clear to this generation. It is no new truth for it is implicit in every page of the New Testament. But the 'evil one', who is ever seeking to sidetrack members of the Church from their true vocation, never succeeds so well as when he gets the idea accepted that the winning of souls is the exclusive concern of bishops and priests, and those members of the laity who have been specially trained for the job. This idea gives the lie to all that is implicit in our Baptism.*

If evangelism is the responsibility of every Christian, the task is much greater than bringing certain methods to bear, however effective:

> *It is important not to get side-tracked in our thinking about Evangelism, so that we fail to see the wood for the trees. We shall never win souls just by discussion groups, nor by techniques of evangelism (visual aids, etc.), nor by better advertising, nor by brighter literature, nor social welfare activities. All these things have their place, but it is very secondary. The sad thing is that the word 'evangelism' so often turns people's minds exclusively to these matters, and before we know where we are, another committee has been set up to discuss 'ways' and 'means'... What is the one thing needful? It is the seeing of evangelism in its right setting. What are we really doing as we strive to turn the eyes of our brother to the light? We are coming into conflict with the powers of darkness who seek to lull men and women into indifference about their eternal destiny. The chief victory of the devil today is that he has got himself taken for granted. We accept as a matter of course the matrimonial chaos, the crimes which fill the daily press, the fear of mankind as we probe the 'nuclear world' and the lust for gold and power which underlies so many economic and racial problems... S. Paul puts the whole matter of evangelism in its right perspective when he says, 'We wrestle not against flesh and blood, but against principalities, against powers, against the rulers of the darkness of this world, against spiritual wickedness in high places.'*

It is prayer and fasting which are the fundamentals to evangelism. Reflecting on saints with a good record on bringing souls to Christ, and naming Saint Francis, Saint Catherine of Siena and Saint Vincent de Paul, Hoey reflects on the ascetic nature of their personal spirituality, in contrast to their outward appearance. *The primary necessity for the conversion of souls, to which our Lord's life and those of his saints bear witness, is prayer and fasting.*

These words show the defining characteristic of Augustine Hoey — that his life is lived and his work undertaken with a constant engagement in the spiritual world. The fruit of his personal prayer is a deep awareness of the presence and reality of God, the angels, the saints and the powers of darkness. A typical Hoey question in discussion about prayer sums this up: *When you say the 'Gloria Patri' don't you feel caught up in the life of God the Holy Trinity?*

Writing about the initial preparations for a Mission, Hoey wrote, *When my religious Superior hands me a letter which reads, 'Dear Father Superior, I should be so glad if you could send me one of your community to consider conducting a mission in my parish...' the first thing to do is to arrange a private visit to the priest concerned... Is the parish priest thinking of the mission as a counsel of despair? — hoping it will make up for his own lack of zeal or pastoral laziness? The first essential to a parish mission is a 'holy' priest, and while few can rise to the heights of a Fr Wainwright or a Curé d'Ars, yet the missioner has every right to expect the vicar to be giving the first claims on his time to prayer, penance and retreat... It is not always easy to say to a brother priest, often older than oneself, 'When did you last go into retreat or make your confession?' but it has to be done.*

Practical common sense was also expected of the priest, and Hoey expresses intolerance of clergy whose service times are arranged around their own convenience but are completely impractical in terms of attracting working people.

Once a Mission was agreed, the next stage would be the Preliminary Visit, allowing for one year's preparation. In the subsequent paragraphs, key priorities in Hoey's vision emerge. He writes that **Prayer** is the most important element. The expectations include the daily Eucharist; use of a mission prayer; a monthly day of prayer; a twenty-four hour vigil; the 'progress' through the parish of crucifixes, and of images or statues of the patron saint; and that a parish retreat be held. Secondly, a programme of **visiting** over five weeks is proposed with 'teaser' cryptic, symbolic leaflets to arouse interest, followed by weekly visits to every home to deliver a series of letters from the parish priest, the bishop, the churchwardens and the Chief Missioner. Detailed notes for visitors are provided, anticipating questions and controversies and suggesting answers. Thirdly, **Publicity** — posters, hoardings, articles in the local press, floodlighting the church, holding outdoor processions. Further practical advice covering everything from arranging a bookstall and managing expenses to arranging cups of tea is included.

For the Mission itself, 'Go Quickly and Tell' sets out a suggested programme for the nightly mission services under 'snap titles' which were a hallmark of the Hoey Mission. The suggested programme includes such titles as "The skeleton in the cupboard i.e. the problem of death", "Psychology excelled i.e. Sacramental Confession" and "The Mother of Millions i.e. Our Lady and the Saints".

Comprehensive guidance is given for the launch and continuation of the mission. The normal order for a mission service is envisaged as community hymn singing — one minute's complete silence — a hymn to the Holy Spirit — notices about the times of services — prayers — first address with biblical readings from a different voice — hymn — second address — short prayer — silence. This is a standard format which any Mirfield mission might have followed. At the end of the services the team are available at the back of church to talk to anyone present.

However, the addresses in a Hoey Mission had a dramatic dimension that went beyond the regular Mirfield mission. The outward aspect of this related to lighting. Hoey's mission address would be given, literally, in the spotlight, with the rest of the church in darkness — he believed that this would aid concentration. The lighting had to be 'blush' since white *would make me look like a corpse.* Hoey later commented that the lighting should not be 'golden' though the mythology of the Hoey Mission has perpetuated the idea of the 'amber' spotlight. Whatever the details, in the words of a member of a mission team years later, "the people were spellbound." This was not merely the result of theatrical production techniques. Hoey's words, demeanour and persona were deeply compelling for the majority of those present, many of whom would never forget him.

For the mission team there was a demanding, some might feel punishing, regime: they were expected to receive holy communion at an early mass, attend the later morning mass as a group, attend a meeting to be allocated visiting duties, conduct the visits, attend a corporate high tea, pray before the mission service and then attend the mission service. Augustine did not expect any more or less from the mission team members than he gave himself. In words reflecting the spirituality and approach of Fr Raymond Raynes, he wrote, *the prayer of the religious life in the Office and the thought of it as a piece of work done for mankind, soon seized me. Even when conducting missions, I never accepted legitimate mitigations, but insisted on the whole of it being recited by the mission team, even though it meant telescoping offices and saying them at absurd times! But I felt the first witness of CR in any mission situation must be to prayer as the source of all our other activities.* Hoey would seclude himself in the afternoons, going over what he would say in his addresses, and appear in Church forty-five minutes before the Mission Service.

At one Mission Service there was a moment of unplanned drama — one which features in Hoey's notes on 'four times when I should have died':

The Community Church at Mirfield

> *I was preaching a fifteen-day mission in the parish of St Mary, South Elmsall (a colliery town in the South Yorkshire coalfield). It was Sunday evening, the last day of the mission, and the church was packed with people sitting in the aisles and in every available corner. I climbed onto the platform from which to preach and began. I had just got well launched when suddenly a large coping stone from one of the pillars came hurtling down. I felt the draught of it as it passed my face and crashed at the foot of the platform where mercifully no-one was sitting. It missed my head by a few inches; otherwise it could easily have killed me. A shudder went through the congregation, but I went straight on preaching as if nothing had happened, although the backs of my legs began to tremble violently. I don't know how I did it, although my legs felt they wanted to give way. However, all was well and a general panic was avoided. It was a frightening experience. I believe it was my Guardian Angel who protected me and indeed other angels who saw to it that the large coping stone fell on the only available small space in the crowded church. It was the sole topic of conversation down the pit the next day!*

Family Missions were an adaptation of the full Mission — the children were taught how to pray in place of receiving instruction on doctrine. A children's mass facing the people with teaching is recommended (a modern idea at the time 'Go Quickly and Tell' was written) and a children's procession at the end of the week. For Youth, the focus was vocation. Of his missions in general, Hoey recalls that it happened very often that *there would be vocations — one new priest and one new religious.*

For a Holy Week and Easter Mission, the dramatic start would be the Stations of the Cross with tableaux around the parish. The recommendations for this suggest full costume and a large cast; roman centurions, banners, sixty to seventy women of Jerusalem. Further tableaux are recommended to illustrate addresses on the Monday, Tuesday and Wednesday of Holy Week and then the Liturgies of the Triduum take on the message. Of the Stations being set up for a

Holy Week Stations of the Cross – Torquay

mission some years later in the parish of Saint Columba's, Sunderland in 1963, Canon Michael Whitehead recalls:

Augustine said, *I think the Women of Jerusalem should come out of that pub there.* I had much to arrange, and forgot to tell my friends at the pub what was planned. In the minutes before the Stations of the Cross began they were bemused... 'There's a whole pile of gypsies coming in!' The Crucifixion was re-enacted outside Church and then the body was carried into Church to Chopin's Dead March, reminiscent of colliery funerals. The body was laid on the altar. The lights went out and there were thunder and lighting effects. A trumpet sounded (played by a police trumpeter, formerly a member of the Household Cavalry) and then Christ was seen risen on top of the altar gradine. The impact was increased by the fact that Christ was played by a newly-Confirmed miner in the congregation. It was all hugely professional.

During one Holy Week, Br Roy CR accompanied Augustine to a parish in Nuneaton for Holy Week and played a full part in the tableaux as Christ. Br Roy had first met Augustine in 1949 at Mirfield. He found that the first impressions of neatness and assurance could be a bit misleading; behind the external appearance he discovered a priest "who can empathise with a range of people from rags to coronets. He had a great personality and enormous imagination and was the best missioner between the 50s and the 80s." He commented that the Holy Week Mission had an enormous impact on the parish. He felt 'worked to death', but Augustine himself never shied away from hard work. (To a member of the team on another mission who mentioned tiredness, Hoey retorted, 'too tired for Him?') However there were tensions at the end of the week when the parish priest commented on the enlargement of his sick communion list, "You come in with a team and leave me to hold things together."

A further recollection is offered by Fr Christopher Jackson:

The Low Church parish I belonged to was asked for help by our neighbouring High Church parish. In the week leading up to Holy Week they were holding a parish mission which would include a procession round the streets and some outdoor preaching; would our Sea Scouts' band be willing to come and play their drums and lead the procession? Friends of mine who were Sea Scouts duly went to rehearsals and came back wide-eyed with tales of what was to happen. Bored with our parish diet of a simple

Communion Service and Evensong I went with others of my age to see what was happening. This must have been around 1963 when Fr Augustine led a mission at St Columba's, Sunderland with outdoor Stations of the Cross: a series of tableaux vivantes acted by parishioners around the streets of Southwick — terraced and council houses occupied by the families of miners, and shipyard workers. The penultimate Station took place just outside of the church when banners displaying the emblems of the Passion (carried by students from the College of the Resurrection) slowly moved aside to reveal the actor playing the part of Christ convincingly nailed to a cross. For the final Station we all crowded into the darkened church, the 'dead' Christ was carried in and placed on the altar prior to a dramatic resurrection with trumpet, organ playing crescendo and lights on. 'I don't think our Vicar would have liked that' observed one of our parishioners.' I didn't think he would have liked it either, but it was marvellous. Not just the drama, but the concept of presenting the Passion to people outside of the church and in the streets where they lived. I can still recall some of Augustine's preaching, when Jesus met his mother (she appeared from the doorway of a pub) and Simon of Cyrene (played by Brother Zachary CR) helped to carry the cross. How many homilies are powerful enough to be remembered fifty years later?

The chapter of 'Go Quickly and Tell' on children's missions focuses on a particular example.

The site could not have been better. It was a large green space right in the central part of the long promenade, just opposite the bus station, where all the day trippers arrived in their coaches. We were there for seven days — a team of twenty-one... Flags, banners and posters decorated the site proclaiming: The Bishop of Durham's Mission to Roker Sands.

The Mission was supported by all the Anglican churches in the town; visiting encompassed public houses and cinemas. It opened with a procession through the town to the mission service at the site, at which the Bishop preached. The team attended the Eucharist in a different church each morning, moving to the marquee for a time of preparation. A children's treasure hunt began at 11.00am and at the end, the children gathered at the marquee for instruction in the faith based on the telling of stories, in which a rabbit and elephant featured.

A team lunch in a restaurant was followed by a procession, led by the 'Holy Family' along the beach at 2.00 p.m. advertising the afternoon service at 3.00 p.m. The theme of the Mission was Christian Marriage and this was explained with tableaux. After high tea for the mission team, handbills and sandwich boards announced the evening mission service at 7.00 p.m., which was instructional in nature, again illustrated by tableaux, on such questions as 'can I believe the Bible?'

Reflecting on the week, Hoey wrote: *This is the type of evangelistic effort for which one can see no immediate results. When one is dealing with large different crowds each day, one cannot attempt to drive them into making definite decisions and resolutions; there are no statistics to prove results, but where the people are, there the Church should be, proclaiming the Word. Some of the seed always takes root, and whatever piece of work is undertaken for God with the right intention, He uses and blesses in his own way. We were given seven days of glorious sunshine which, on that part of the north-east coast, is always a miracle in itself.*

'Go Quickly and Tell' ends with a chapter on how the plans for the 'follow up' need as much prayer, thought and planning as the preparation. The whole point and purpose of the Mission is to gather in the harvest afterwards. The emphasis is on maintaining key elements of the mission — daily Eucharist with good attendance, prayer, retreats and visiting.

Here, however, a note of caution needs to be sounded. In some parishes, the Mission marked only a temporary spiritual revival, while in others, Catholic practices such as the daily Eucharist and Confession could be renewed only to be swept away with a change of Vicar. These uncertainties lie behind Hoey's relatively recent reflection on, and severe assessment of, his work in conducting such missions: *It was a complete waste of time.*

* * *

In July 1953 Augustine was appointed Warden of Hemingford Grey, the Mirfield retreat house in Cambridgeshire south of Huntingdon. He chose a lot of the furnishings, and prided himself that the carpets he had chosen lasted the whole of CR's tenure of the house; there was also the project to convert cottages into rooms for retreatants. For his monthly visits to Hemingford Grey, Augustine would have travelled by train from Mirfield to Huntingdon, taking a taxi to the village or being met by the ex-Navy Lady Warden, Gwen Holsford, whom he described as 'smitten with Raymond Raynes who to her was God.' Hoey found her very demanding. He held the position until 1958, just after being sent abroad. (A later memory shared by Fr Antony Grant CR was of a subsequent Lady Warden, 'the redoubtable Mrs Somers Smith, who Fr Clifford Green CR used to say came to answer the door wearing a white veil with a glass of gin in one hand and a cigarette in another.')

From 3 January 1956, Augustine was Director of the Fraternity of the Resurrection (FR). In 1903 the CR Quarterly Journal explained that 'an association has been formed, called the 'Fraternity of the Resurrection' consisting of those who wish to be connected with the Community and to share in its work. It is hoped that the Quarterly may be the organ of that Association. The members of the Fraternity are incorporated into and associated with the Community according to the degree of their commitment. The Fraternity is, therefore, an integral part of the family of the Community and is animated by the same dedication of the mystery of the Resurrection. Members of the Fraternity work together to build up common life in the various communities, groups and families to which they belong.'

Augustine described carrying out the role as being somewhat akin to the life of a travelling salesman. He felt he was always on the move, particularly when carrying out a tour of the many branches of FR on the south coast, staying one night in each place. Under his guidance, pilgrimages to Walsingham and Assisi were introduced. A note from FR documents of 1956 captures the sense of pain at Christian divisions that is a hallmark of Hoey's spirituality: *The week of prayer for Christian Unity. The Community is pledged to work and pray for the reunion of Christendom. Each member of the FR ought to be a centre of unity, radiating the charity of Christ in his own sphere; that charity which is implicit in the Risen Lord's greeting and gift of 'Peace'. Unity is primarily a matter of the spiritual life. Let all members try to be at Mass daily; there is much to be said for attending Eucharistic Worship as interpreted in other denominations, during the week of prayer — Nonconformist, Orthodox, Roman — refraining from communicating, in sorrow and reparation for our unhappy divisions and all the blood which has been shed in past centuries in the name of orthodoxy.* Retreats were also encouraged: *The sooner we get rid of the idea that retreats are only for pious people the better, for surely every regular communicant should spend one or two days a year in the kind of silence which will help them to hear God.* Also in 1956 it was announced that two thirds of the royalties from "Naught for your Comfort" by Trevor Huddleston CR would be donated to the development and expansion of the school at Penhalonga, South Africa. In 1957 Fr Hilary Beasley CR took over as Director of the Fraternity.

With a five-year programme of Missions in full swing Augustine relates an event that changed his direction. *I was summoned one evening after Compline to see the Superior, Raymond Raynes, who asked, "Is there any family or particular reason why you should not go to South Africa?" I couldn't say there was…*

chapter 5

Africa

I WAS ANXIOUS at the Superior's question, 'Is there any family or particular reason why you should not go to South Africa?' I remember wondering what my parents would think. But it was inevitable because it is in the Rule. I asked, what about the 5-year programme of missions I had planned...?"

After six months, Fr Augustine sailed from Southampton on a boat acting as Chaplain to the children on board for two weeks. At an early stage in the journey Hoey relates: *I lost my heart to Madeira where we had six hours ashore. It was the Feast of the Immaculate Conception so that the churches both inside and out were a riot of decoration and electrical illumination — not tawdry but really beautiful.*

The ship docked in Cape Town and Hoey travelled by train to Johannesburg, a journey which took thirty six hours. He paid for the luxury train — this was not approved of by the Brethren. He was met by a crowd led by Fr George Sidebotham CR.

In a letter to Members of the Fraternity of the Resurrection written a few weeks after his arrival, Hoey gives an account of the journey aboard ship.

Priory of Christ the King,
74 Meyer Street,
Sophiatown,
Johannesburg

March 1958

It seems a very long time since I left Southampton in the thick fog of early December. The boat was packed and soon became a little world all of its own as, after leaving Madeira, we saw no land for ten days. It was like a microcosm of the big world in so far as the majority had not the least interest in religion — and as I was the only Anglican priest on board, I did at times feel as if I was living in some kind of ivory tower! Fortunately there were two coloured nurses returning after training in England. One had worked for the St Peter's sisterhood at Woking and the other was brought up at our church here and lives only a mile away. They both provided me with a daily Mass congregation. I had quite a decent altar set up daily amid the blue silk cushions and gilt-legged furniture of the First Class Library and I had taken vestments with me. The Masses were advertised in all parts of the ship. On Sundays we rose to fourteen but most weekdays it was just the two nurses — and there were over six hundred passengers! A group of Romans came eagerly to me the first day but were not quite so eager once they discovered who I was. They had no priest, so the three German and two Irish nuns had no spiritual ministrations for a fortnight. These nuns were very friendly to me and the German ones made a point of asking how many had been at "your Holy Mass, Father". I talked until I was nearly silly on the religious life, for one after another, as they got to know me, were curious and wanted to know who, what and why I was.

Departing for South Africa

So I hope I did some good but my two cabin mates were quite impervious, as far as I could see, to all my leading questions. One of them was like a stage version of the Wild West: tall, lean, bristling beard and a passion for check shirts. He was, in fact, a South African but bitten with the wanderlust. He had travelled all round the world — though only 32 — just goes to the next place he fancies, gets a job (electronics) and having saved enough to get to the next place, goes! I discovered he had been Confirmed in Jo'burg Cathedral, but every time I brought up the question of his religion he used to get so red and embarrassed that finally I desisted. The other was a photographer from Streatham, who visits the game reserves here every year — treks through them alone with a camera and a tent, photographing the animals and sells the results at high prices to firms which specialise in educational publishing. He was only 30 but, being half French, had a background of lapsed Romanism (his mother). He was a friendly soul but had not the slightest interest in religion. I don't think any of the three of us were sorry when we reached Capetown! I hope the 'bearded one' will marry a tidy wife; I have met many people who flourish in chaos but he excelled them. At the end of fourteen days, every peg, drawer and shelf in the cabin was draped with his clothes and he even hung a line across the cabin — his socks and shoes were scattered all over the floor, his notepaper, bottles of ink, bathing costumes and empty sherry bottles found their way on to all our bunks. I used to lie on my bunk and watch his various garments swaying and sagging on the line and think it would make a marvellous 'set' for some play about slums!

I didn't think the Head Waiter had much imagination about the way he placed us at tables. I had a nice bright young thing from Liverpool at my side, determined to get everything she could out of the trip — she ought to have had some nice bright eligible young man beside her (there were some) but, instead, she got me! Opposite was a raw, shy Scottish lad of 15 from Glasgow, going out to join his father who has an engineering job in Rhodesia. His accent was so broad I could rarely tell what he said.

In addition to me and the nuns, the other professional religious passengers were: 1) a nice but narrow Methodist Minister and his wife who have worked for many years in S. Rhodesia — each night they sat in one of the lounges playing some spelling game and drinking lemonade and would have had me with them, but I only obliged twice; 2) a Plymouth Brethren Minister and wife, who took me on one side and gave me a long lecture, with Bible quotations, on the evils of drink, after they had seen me sharing a bottle of wine with someone at dinner! And 3) six raw Canadian male Seventh Day Adventists, all very young and bursting with immature zeal. They steered clear of me as they formed their little huddle on deck, always with their Bibles in hand. One of them ventured to ask my interpretation of a certain passage in the Gospels over which they had apparently been quarrelling. I gave the Catholic one and they never asked again. I think it is the Kelloggs breakfast food which have the Seventh Day Adventists as their chief shareholder, so next time you pile your plate high with what the packet describes as 'sun-drenched flakes', just remember you are helping young men such as I met to come and increase the religious confusion in this country.

You will see that I had plenty of cause on the voyage to meditate both on the paganism of the age and the frustrations of the divisions of Christendom. It made me feel I had been living in a fool's paradise for years, but I survived. One bright spot was that everyone had heard of Fr Huddleston and his book was on sale in the "tourist" shop and I saw lots reading it.

Sophiatown is much as I expected it to be although no-one had prepared me for the wonderful and moving singing of African people in Church. It is something out of this world. The ghastly political situation and, especially, the results of apartheid, are ever with me. In fact, they drown, swamp and cloud all one's thinking, until I begin to realise I have never in my life had to live so close to evil. It is hard to have to watch people suffering, shouted at, despised, denied justice, bereft of freedom, treated like animals and all because of the colour of their skin — harder to stand by and know there is nothing one can do materially. It is the vocation of Our Lady at the Cross which is needed, to stand and watch and know one can only bring spiritual weapons to the conflict. But that is not easy.

An old African woman standing outside her house with her possessions around her, waiting to be taken 16 miles away, because Sophiatown has been declared a European area (she had lived here all her life) said to me, "Father, why are we treated like flies? It's a puff here and a puff there and off we go!" Why indeed? This kind of thing can breed nothing but deep hatred and bitterness, especially among a people who are still for the most part semi-heathen. There is trouble coming to this land in a big way. In fact, I feel much like a Christian living in ancient Rome, for so many of the Europeans are victims to the gold lust, intent only on their lovely houses, their exotic gardens and private swimming pools. They are paganised to the n'th degree and refuse to listen to any Christian talk about racial relationships — it is incredible that in spite of so many of the outward trappings of civilisation, they treat the African as a slave who is there to make living easy and convenient — but who can be a nuisance and therefore it is important to keep a pistol in the bedside drawer, just in case he gets nasty. I suppose the citizens of ancient Rome felt much the same about their slave population.

I shall never forget my arrival in Jo'burg. For nearly 24 hours the train seemed to have been moving across open country with scattered farms here and there and then, suddenly there loomed up on the horizon this city with its skyscrapers. It is very brash, none of it more than sixty years old, and it really looks like a vast American advertisement for steel and concrete. All round the city, thrusting up into the sky, are the great yellow mine dumps, which almost glitter in the brilliant sunshine and are a perpetual reminder that this place had its origin in the lust for gold. Nothing counts here except money and some people have lots and lots of it — but where a place has no other tradition than that of gold, the materialism is a live, evil thing, which hits one in the eyes and grips the soul every time one walks down one of the crowded glaring concrete streets. It is seen in the typical European woman who goes out shopping as if dressed for a Royal Garden Party! Little wonder that this country produces so few vocations either to the priesthood or the religious life — materialism plus the prevailing racial policy cloud thinking and belittle any idea of a life of sacrifice.

Materialism alone does not do it, for few countries are more materialistic than America, yet there is no shortage of vocations there to the cloister and the priesthood. I am painting a dark picture, but I am sure it is not exaggerated. There is a group of Europeans who are liberally minded politically (especially the Jews) and who have an interest in 'culture', but they are a small minority in a vast country. We tend to come into contact with them a lot because of our racial tolerance, but it is no use pretending that they are as yet an effective political force. Even if the present Government, which so closely resembles Nazism in its views and methods, is thrown out at the next election in April, which is doubtful, the only other party (the United Party) is no great improvement. It will be more laissez-faire in racial matters but all its tenets are based on the White Supremacy. However, it would provide a breathing space and the worst aspects of native persecution would cease.

In view of all this evil and wrong-thinking, I think the best news for the Christians in this country is the multi-racial foundation which the Sisters of the Precious Blood are making in Basutoland. It is the first Anglican contemplative order to open a house overseas. Eight of the sisters have left Burnham Abbey, Maidenhead, to form the basis of this foundation and already there are African postulants and novices. It is a real work of sacrifice for those eight nuns who will never see England again. But the life of prayer which will be carried on at their new Convent of Our Lady of Mercy in Basutoland will be far more effective in undermining the evil of this country than any amount of political speaking and 'active' work. "We wrestle not," says St Paul, "against flesh and blood, but against the spiritual hosts of wickedness." The problem must be dealt with at this level. It is hidden lives of prayer which have a mighty influence. Like the yeast in the dough or the seed growing secretly in the ground — and so this new little convent is at the very centre of the age-old strife between the powers of darkness and light in this country and, as far as I see things, is the only star in a very black night. One of the things I am looking forward to most is being able to visit this new community. It is several hundred miles from here in a remote and mountainous part of Basutoland, but as our Provincial, Fr Sidebotham, is acting as their Warden, I hope to be able to go with him, by car, on one of his visits. The more I think about the work of the enclosed Orders, the more I am driven to the conclusion that they matter most to the conversion of the world. We need an Anglican one for men very badly. This is something we pray about at Mirfield every week and the late bishop of Oxford, Dr. Kirk, said it was one of his greatest hopes for the Church of England. Please keep this in your prayers. The fact that no form of the monastic life earns such scorn, hatred and misunderstanding from the 'world' is the surest proof of its value — for the Devil knows it and therefore he must do his utmost to destroy them.

Here in the Priory of Christ the King, we really act as parish priests to a vast African parish and to me, in many ways, it is like going back to the early days of my priesthood in Hackney Wick. There are all the same things to be done: the sick and dying to be cared for, people to be visited and prepared for the Sacraments and children to be taught (the average length of Confirmation classes is fifteen months!). It is a hindrance not knowing the native language and always being at the mercy of interpreters — one is never sure they have said what one meant! I am in charge of St Francis Church which is amid a vast squalid clutter of African homes, built out of corrugated iron sheets and anything else they can lay their hands on to keep the rain off their heads. St Francis is the only solid and decent building. It is difficult to describe it inside — to European eyes it is a bit of a nightmare. The Africans love bright colours and tinsel, so it is an absolute riot of the cheapest, crudest images and pictures. There is St Joseph with a wreath of pink roses round his head, looking so astonished at finding this tribute fastened on him; a chocolate-faced Our Lady with large earrings; another icing-sugar version of Our Lady of Fatima presides over the font; banners of St Peter and St Michael liberally spattered with sequins and glass jewels; and a smiling St Francis caressing some enormous doves. At Christmas, in the crib, both Our Lady and St Joseph wore paper crowns from the inside of crackers, while the Holy Child was wrapped in a little patchwork quilt. But it all represents real devotion and it is a moving experience to sing Mass there amid the roar of African singing. All the shrines are cluttered with brass vases — and the African doesn't mind whether flowers are alive or dead. He will bring quite dead flowers and arrange them with great care and love around the tabernacle. I have to shut my eyes to it all and carry on.

I expect that you have read that under the Group Areas Act many of our parishioners are being forcibly moved away but even if the scheme is completed, it will leave us with at least half the population in another part of the parish, so there will still be lots for us to do.

I have done some outside work, mainly retreats. When one goes across to the other side of the city to do some white work, it is like stepping into another world. It is almost unbelievable that such contrasts in the way of living can exist side by side. The European, on the whole, is not concerned about the African way of life; it is a closed shop to him, but the African knows all about European living; he watches it with envious eyes from the servants' quarters of the house where he works and he grows in silent determination to have it all for himself one day.

Thank you for the constant support of your prayers. I am always conscious of them and they have helped me to slip easily into a situation which is very different from what I have been used to during the last seven years of conducting missions. I am very glad of the opportunity of sharing the life of CR here.

Please remember me in Holy Week when I am being sent to preach the Passion in one of the more prosperous European suburbs (St Augustine's, Orange Grove). Then, 28th April to 3rd May, I conduct the Wantage Sisters' retreat, 11th to 15th May the Whitby Sisters' retreat and on the 6th July I do the first broadcast ever from one of the churches in the town at Evensong, but all these things are merely incidental to the busy life of this parish.

I try to remember you at the altar and I do hope you will have much joy in the coming Paschal Feast and that you will pray that we may be used to thrown some of the Light of the Resurrection into the darkness of this troubled country.

Christ (sic) *regnat. Alleluia. Yours affectionately in Xto,*
Augustine Hoey. CR

The Superior at Mirfield, Fr Raymond Raynes had said, "it would be better if you go to Rosettenville to lead missions for white people." However, the letter reveals that this was not how things worked out. Looking back at the period, Hoey reflects that *South Africa was a shock. The priory was alright but set amid squalor.* He appreciated the traditional English Anglo-Catholicism with a strong sense of God and the 'other'. The problems faced included drunkenness — people drank all their wages — and Hoey became used to drunken bodies in the church doorway on Saturday nights, indeed *grew to love them. The children were marvellous — three hundred of them in church could be silent and there was no problem about discipline.*

Hoey in later life reflected *I became very anti-white and was considered pro-black. I could not preach about race — we had to keep as quiet as we could.* His own perception is of considerable affinity and good relationships with black Africans. The mythology in the Community of the Resurrection is at odds with this as expressed by Fr Dominic Whitnall, CR, in a comment echoed by other brethren at Mirfield: "Augustine couldn't gel with Africans. His manner didn't work. He was unable to get beyond outward colour with SOME and could come across as tactless."

Back at Mirfield, Fr Jonathan Graham CR became Superior and moved Hoey to Sukkukunhiland Priory set in a tribal area with responsibility for the Jane Furse Hospital. *I felt helpless there. Few could speak English outside the Hospital. I was responsible for ten villages out in the Bund with dirt roads and mountains. Preaching was with interpreters in three languages.* Hoey relates an anecdote about Fr Dennis Shropshire CR, a scholar somewhat lacking in common sense. He started a sermon on the Athanasian Creed. The interpreter translated this as "Father wishes you good morning!" One had to speak in short sentences.

* * *

St Francis Priory,
PO Jane Furse Hospital,
via Middleburg, N. Transvaal.

October 1958

The scene has changed considerably since I last wrote for, as you know, I have been appointed Prior of this House. Before I wrote from the 'concrete jungle' of Johannesburg, but here we are in the heart of the country and sixty miles from the nearest town. Range upon range of hills loom up against the sky in every direction, changing their colours at every hour of the day and giving the impression of tremendous spaciousness and stillness, which is a wonderful change after Sophiatown where the nights were punctuated by the shrieks of young people, the barking of half-starving dogs and the throb of incessant [Zionist] drum-beating! When Fr Sidebotham, our Provincial, drove me here and the car turned aside from the main road, to sand roads which seemed to plunge straight into the hills, I thought to myself, "this is more the kind of African which one associated with the missionary magazine's of one's childhood!" Occasionally we passed mud kraals, with the families squatting with the goats against the walls, or there would loom up against the sky the figure of a woman walking with such slow and beautiful grace, balancing on her head an enormous water pot and her baby tied on her back. Approaching each village gave one rather a jolt for there at the entrance was a row of huts, of identical size, side by side, each with a cross on the roof and proclaiming themselves over the door, 'Catholic', 'Anglican', 'Lutheran', 'Bantu Methodist', 'Apostolic', 'Dutch Reform' and so on... It is a sad reflection of the way in which we have brought the Faith to this country and it is precisely this division which prompts the African to be ever 'breaking away', usually due to some miserable quarrel or desire to be a religious leader, and founding some new religious group. There are two thousand African sects in this country at the moment, all calling themselves 'Christian', which is an appalling thought and ought to stir even the most lethargic member of the Church to make reparation in urgent prayer for unity.

The Chapel, June Furse Hospital

Yet in spite of this medley of religious meeting houses in each village this part of Africa is still predominantly heathen. As yet not a single chief has embraced Christianity, perhaps because they don't want to restrict themselves to only one wife! But in a primitive, tribal society one has to be very strong-minded to 'go a different way' from the chief, which perhaps explains why such Anglicans as there are tend to be the better-educated and finer type of African. Witchcraft and superstition haunt the people, so there is plenty of elemental evil lurking around and at night when vivid lightning flashes on the hills for hours and the faint throbbing of drums or heathen chanting can be heard on the still air, the effect is almost 'pantomime' and at any moment one expects the trap door to open and the devil to jump out!

The astonishing thing is that in the midst of all this stands the modern Jane Furse Hospital, having the latest in equipment and ever expanding. The heathen, primitive people flock to it in increasing numbers, all their fears about it having been broken down. They know it is a Christian hospital and they listen or take part quite cheerfully in the daily ward prayers, but when they are better, they leave all the shining efficiency and their hospital bed and return without a qualm to their mud hut, the floor to sleep on and their heathen customs...

This is a mission hospital, drawing grants from the S.P.G. (Society for the Propagation of the Gospel) But alas! We have been compelled to accept government grants in order to expand, which means our position is precarious. The government has no love of the Church and we only have to

make one wrong step in the 'apartheid racket' and they will step in and commandeer the lot and 'out' we shall have to go. It is terrible to be dependent on them for money, but Anglicans have generally so little sacrificial sense of almsgiving that we have been jockeyed into this position. Can you imagine the R.C.'s letting a hospital 'go' through lack of money? We have much to learn from them in this matter. With the nationalist government riding in triumph and all African schools having been wrested from religious bodies, it is only a matter of time before African mission

Clockwise: Luke, Derek, Augustine, Stephen

hospitals will have to go the same way. In the meantime we carry on and comfort ourselves with the truth that governments do fail and totter!

I need not stress the sacrificial side. The isolation of the hospital, the tensions of too much to do and living on top of one another, with no town amenities for one's 'day off'. I can only quote that greatest of all missionaries, St Francis Xavier, "all these things turn to refreshment and consolation when borne for Him to whom our duty is absolute." So ask yourself if the attractive picture of Christ moving among the sick in the Gospel narratives is not seeking to make its claim on your life?

We are four fathers in this Priory. Myself and Frs. Carter, Smith and Williams. Fr Carter has spent the entire forty years of his professed life in this country. Now at 73 with vast flowing white beard and shaggy hair, with carved African walking stick and sun helmet, he is like some Old Testament figure, not the thundering prophet type, but gracious and full of sympathy and love. Fr Smith was in the noviciate with me and is about two years older. He is a great gardener and our Priory garden, which falls away in a series of steps and terraces from our cloister, is a riot of exotic colour. It is watered by a series of cunningly devised concrete tanks under the steps of the terraces which catch and store every drop of the precious rain... for this is 'a barren and a dry land where no water is.' He is a great linguist and when he goes off for a few days to some of our district churches, of which there are nine, he will speak nothing but the native tongue. Fortunately it is my job to remain here at the centre where English is understood. Fr Williams is very young, only one year in profession, and so happily has all the zeal and energy necessary to cycle 10 miles along some tortuous rocky mountainous sand track to a district Church... say Mass... and cycle back smiling to ask for more! He too is picking up the language well. I hope these bits of information will help you to pray for us better... and pray too that I may be given the gift of 'wisdom' for the matron suddenly divulged last week that the Chaplain always gives a course of 12 lectures on Nursing Ethics (!) to those in training. I ran my eye down the list with some anxiety: such subjects as 'Relationship of nurses to doctors'. How can I last out for one hour in saying, "It is unprofessional for nurses to attempt to flirt with the doctors or to be disobedient to his professional demands!"

The dark shadow of the Nationalist Government is always with us, just as acutely as in the city. Within the hospital we have to obey the madness of apartheid e.g. the Indian doctor is not allowed to give any kind of order or instruction to a white nurse. In the district there have been endless killings, murders, arrests and deportations of chiefs during recent months because people resisted the government's will for them. Things are quieter now and some of the chiefs are being allowed to return...

I am writing this as the Feast of St Francis draws near, under whose patronage we live in this Priory. Unfortunately I am in bed with jaundice which is not the way I should have chosen to begin the rule of this House!

* * *

Hoey recalls his disappointment that although there were
Lutherans and Catholics he never really felt that he had made contact
with them. He looked after four Daughters of Mary — black nuns
with no English who had faced great opposition, and who feature in
his next circular letter home.

* * *

April 1959

*On all sides we are beset by the most flagrant injustice and everything is
sacrificed to the myth of white supremacy. At the moment there is untold
suffering over the implementing of racial theories. Every African must
belong to his own tribe, even though he may have lost touch with them for
two generations and become completely urbanised... yet he must ""put the
clock back" in his life. If he happens to be married to a coloured woman,
then he must leave her, for African must marry African, otherwise he breaks
the law. In Capetown an African of 60 married for 30 years to a coloured
woman — six children — was told he must leave and return to his tribe.
She was then turned out of their shack with the younger children, sent to a
"coloured area" where the African husband was forbidden entrance. So it
goes on, the ruthless destruction of home life...It leave one speechless with
indignation — and it seems to me that we Christians are compromising all
along the line. We stand on the sidewalks, wringing our hands and groaning
"how terrible", but we do nothing that might get our names put on those
black lists kept in the files of government offices... Jane Furse is in a native
reserve and Europeans only live here on government sufferance and can be
turned out at 2 months' notice. Does one turn a blind eye to the injustices
and misery of apartheid regulations and get on with the work of healing,
or protest against them and be turned out. It is a difficult question and one
which we all tend to shelve... Nevertheless, I can't help reflecting that the
early Christians went to the lions rather than bow to the common social
custom demanded by the government (but which nobody took very seriously)
of burning a pinch of incense before the statue of the Emperor.*

*Since I last wrote I have been on pilgrimage to the grave of our local
child martyr, Manche Masemola. She was flogged to death by her parents
30 years ago for attending Baptism classes. They were frightened when they
discovered what they had done and so buried her some miles out of their
village — but the Christians soon discovered the place and it became a place
of pilgrimage. It is in the heart of the bush and her bones lie under a large
rock round which cacti have been planted and grown to a height of 20 feet, so
that they form an impenetrable wall to the little sanctuary... It was very hot*

the day I went with Father Smith and Sister Sophia O.H.P.; we managed to get the truck jolting and jarring along the most terrible road to within two miles of the grave but then had to scramble the rest of the way over rocks. When we got there we sang the Te Deum and put candles on the grave. The silence was intense and the humming of insects only seemed to intensify the stillness. We were just settling down to Sext, when a hornet came straight at me like a dive bomber, leaving its sting in the middle of my nose... a very unpleasant sensation. Little did I know it but at the same time a tick was climbing my leg and injected its deadly poison into my thigh, which a short time afterwards developed into a raging bout of tick fever, which laid me low for three weeks — so I consider I paid very highly for my devotion to our martyr. However, nothing daunted, I have persuaded the Bishop to lead a big pilgrimage next February during the Octave of the martyrdom and to say Mass at the shrine.

Also in Marishane there came into being about the time of Manche's death a community of African nuns who call themselves the Daughters of Mary. It is as remarkable thing that five young girls in the midst of heathenism should have heard and followed the call to the religious life in their own local village...where they have lived in vows for over 20 years. The opposition and persecution they endured, not least from their own families, was terrific for chastity is not a thing admired or understood by African Christians — let alone the heathen. Daughters represent money, for a suitor always has to pay a handsome sum in either cash or cattle to the family from which he takes his bride. The parents of these girls tried to demand payment from the church for 'stealing their daughters'. It was not paid... We are only able to get to their village for Mass once a week, otherwise they have to manage on their own. I try to give them a devotional talk once a month, but it has to be done through an interpreter because not one of them can speak a word of English — so one is terribly limited because much of the devotional thinking and expression of Western Europe just cannot be translated into the local dialect...

We had a tragedy in our midst a month ago when the local native commissioner shot himself. All these commissioners are Europeans, very tough: they have to be for it is their job to carry out the government decrees on the Africans. No-one with a Christian conscience could do such a job. This particular one was of Greek extraction and found himself more and more troubled about doing the things his superiors expected of him — Sekhukuniland being the most rebellious of all the country districts in the peoples' opposition to government policy, ruthlessness was expected of the commissioner in his dealings with them. He started to be lenient. The native affairs department had wind of it and brought increasing pressure on him until he was driven to suicide. He was brought to the hospital but there wasn't much I could do as he was unconscious. The bullet was lodged in his brain. We have not got the people here who could cope with the skilful operation to remove it — so with frantic telephoning we managed to get him an air-lift to Pretoria. But the bullet was too deeply embedded to be extracted and he died 48 hours later without regaining consciousness. I was reminded once again of Nazi Germany where many officials committed suicide when the sinful nature of their work began to pray on their minds... One of the shocking side lights of this tragedy was that the controlled Press did not report it as suicide — but made out that he had been shot by an African — just to increase European antagonism to these "treacherous natives". It does infuriate one and one feels so helpless.

* * *

The grip of the Government over the churches and the tightening of apartheid continued, as we read in Hoey's next letters.

* * *

November 1959

As the Anglican Church is stripped one by one of all her African institutions — and as we see the injustices, the broken and miserable and poverty-stricken fate of the African people groaning beneath the Cross of apartheid and white supremacy, so it is true that the Passion of Christ is being wrought again in them. No words of mine can depict this suffering which hems us in on all sides and the indignity of seeing people persecuted and harried brutally and cruelly because they do not happen to have a white skin...

The Prophets of the Old Testament are read aloud in church but it is easy to forget that the very things they inveighed against are still with us in the conditions under which the African and coloured people live. The violent contrast between extreme wealth and utter poverty, the social injustices, the starvation, the homelessness, these are the things at which the average European shrugs his shoulders. "Don't let us talk about the situation," said a wealthy woman to me in one of Jo'burg's rich houses, "it's too awful." So we talked about her dog instead, which she had shampooed and manicured at one of the city's exclusive pet salons at the price of two guineas per week! I am sure some good white communicants are beginning to think about these things , but they fear the ostracism of their neighbours if they begin to treat Africans as people and try to meet them socially.

This may seem a grim letter, more akin to the spirit of Holy Week than the forthcoming festival of the Nativity. That is not so — for if the shades of the Passion are beginning to close around the Church in this country, the same shadow falls across the Manger as one contemplates the Divine Child, unwanted and cast out by his fellow men, enduring the hard wood of the Manger, the constriction of the swaddling bands, the darkness and the cold. The Manger and the Cross are one and we cannot forget it, nor shall we as we offer the Midnight Mass.

But there are brighter things, for we have just presented seventy candidates for Confirmation, which is 'history' in Sekhukhuniland for there has never been anything like this number before.

* * *

May 1960

Here at Jane Furse all is quiet on the surface and the daily routine goes on much as usual. We have had the police snooping around, but if they found anything that came under the term 'subversive' they are as yet keeping quiet about it. The newest bit of legislation, that anyone not South African can be deported without any kind of appeal or redress opens up many possibilities! It means that 95% of our community could be swept out of the country at a moment's notice. So does the pressure increase to keep us all 'good boys'! there is so much on all sides to turn one's thoughts to Hitler's Germany...

Nurses with Hoey at the Jane Furse Hospital

We must do our utmost to secure social righteousness and justice but in the end we have here no abiding city and Our Lord never at any time said we should have peace on earth. In fact He suggests the reverse, for parable after parable makes clear that when the Truth is proclaimed men will begin to take sides — division and hostility will ensue and so it will be 'until He comes again' at the end of all things. Even when Our Lord was dying on the Cross he created a division of opinion among his two companions on either side. 'The one shall be taken and the other left' — these words present us with a great mystery. I only say this because I think we can only get a right sense of proportion about the various efforts of the powers of darkness to destroy Christian Truth throughout the ages by realising that the Gospels do not tell us that the end will be when all believe, but when all have had a chance to believe. When the Gospel has been preached to all nations then we can begin to expect the second Coming and all that this expectation means to us in the way of joy and gladness. In the meantime we can expect the kind of situation in which the Church finds herself faced in this country and if it was not this particular manifestation against which we can hurl our darts of ultimate victory, then it would be another. Racial persecution is no new thing. Sometimes people write from England as if we were on the verge of martyrdom and almost in the jaws of the lions. Well, that may be so, but it only appears like that because the ideas are clear cut. I doubt whether it is fundamentally very different in England, or would not be if the Truth was really proclaimed by the Church. But in times when, as Mr Macmillan said, "so many have never had it so good", there is bound to be a latent materialism, seeping into the soul, blighting and blunting the Christian conscience — so that for those who have eyes to see the devil is just as rampant, only more subtly than in South Africa. I am glad to read of the great public demonstrations being made against apartheid in England — but I also know that unless those who shout loudest are in their own individual lives striving to love their neighbour as themselves, no spiritual energy can be released by it, nor much permanent good be achieved.

* * *

Hoey went on to describe his experience while preaching a Lenten Mission in Northern Rhodesia...

* * *

It was curious seeing the copperbelt only through European eyes because owing to the language difficulties the missions were preached mainly to 'whites'. As I moved from one house to another or stood in the pulpit I had to pinch myself to realise that I was not in Epsom or some other outer London suburb and to remember that somewhere in the background there were thousands of Africans! Most of the few Africans I saw were those behind the kitchen door or handing me sandwiches on silver trays.

In Luanshya, where about a dozen Africans came each night to the mission service and afterwards came into the parish hall with the Europeans to tea, one of the white women came to see me about it. She was the wife of an artisan at the mine. "It can't be right," she said, "for these natives to see us Europeans waiting on them with cups of tea. Where is it going to end? Why, my own garden boy might be among them and how humiliated he would be if I was to wait on him with tea and cake!" I remonstrated, but nothing I could say altered her attitude and in the end she got quite edgy and said, "Oh you Anglican priests are all the same" — which I regarded as quite a compliment for ecclesia anglicana. It is easy to be indignant with her, but the real problem is how to change her heart. Within a tight, white circle her life was full of Christianity. The mission had a profound effect on her and yet she completely missed the one thing needful. She is typical of the problem except for the fact that she was a much nicer, more generous person than many of her co-Europeans. But it puts many questions to one's own conscience as one mounts the pulpit: ought one to thunder forth racial truths — in which case the church would be empty the next night? Or just go on with the normal proclamation of the Faith, as on a mission in England, hoping that the dawn will break on the darkness in their hearts?

* * *

28 October 1960

It is quite useless being daunted by the difficulties , for the Gospel promises that 'in the world ye shall have tribulation…' and if the Community is being driven to live a day at a time, stripped of its works one by one and unable to plan any kind of future, what does it matter? The shades of the Passion should not overwhelm us, for we know the ultimate victory is ours.…

Sunday October 9th was a day of great heat — a hot wind, a blazing sun and because the rains are late this year, clouds and clouds of choking dust. We were due to leave the Priory at 7.00am, which by 'African time' means any time between 7 and 8. It was exactly 7.45am when we moved off, a long convoy of trucks, bus and private cars all lurching and churning up a great dust storm. I was in our local African bus which we had hired, a bus which must have been cast on the scrap heap before our local African bought it! And that it goes at all or even holds together is a great tribute to the angels. We were packed like sardines, both standing and sitting. It took three to drive the bus, one at the wheel, one astride the engine catching in a tin the perpetual leaking oil from a broken pipe and a third with a large bucket of water to given repeated 'drinks' to the radiator. At every hill the bus groaned, filled up with foul-smelling blue smoke and expired and nothing would induce it to go until, amid clouds of steam, water was put in the radiator! It took us 1 hour 45 minutes to do 26 miles and at one point we skidded in the sand, ran up the bank and hovered perilously for a moment and finally decided to come down the right way up. The bus passengers were not in the least perturbed — to them it seemed a very normal journey.

Leaving our transport behind we began to walk in silent procession to the grave — the crucifer leading, then the Bishop with his crozier and about 300 of us panting behind. It was very hot as we toiled for a mile over the rocks and I was very glad the bishop had given us a dispensation about fasting: nothing for 3 hours before Communion, which meant that we had all had something before 7.00am. Finally we got to the grave to find other people waiting for us. The trees planted round the grave form the walls of a natural little chapel and these were all hung with beautiful wreaths of flowers woven by the African nuns (the Daughters of Mary) who had been playfellows of Manche. We set up an altar and the Bishop began the Mass for a Virgin Martyr.

There are some kinds of religious experiences which defy being put into words and this was one of those: even the children seemed wide-eyed with awe and the silence was intense, broken only by the murmur of insects. Some people are more susceptible to atmospheres than others, but anyone who has visited Manche's grave is always caught by the fact that it is a 'holy place'. Some time ago a group of people went intending to sing Evensong, but as they knelt on arrival they were so 'gripped' by the 'feel' of the place, that they remained in silence for half an hour and then crept away. After Mass the congregation filed through the shrine kneeling in twos and threes in silent prayer at the grave. So ended one of the most moving religious experiences I have ever had since setting foot in this troubled land — but not just for me alone, for everyone. The people have talked of nothing else since and the Bishop was so thrilled that he wants us to institute the Pilgrimage as an annual diocesan occasion and has instructed us to get a proper and permanent altar built over the grave for next year... It is to be my duty to bring up the 'cause' of Manche at our next Diocesan Synod in January so that we can get her day observed throughout the Diocese with the Bishop's imprimatur.

* * *

Hoey's task of introducing to the Diocesan Synod, the 'cause' of the martyr Manche Masemola, reached its culmination in 1975, long after his time in South Africa, when the Church of the Province of South Africa added her name to its liturgical calendar. She is commemorated on 4th February as a martyr. When, in 1928, it became clear to her that her parents would oppose her desire for Baptism and fearful that the beatings she received for attending baptism classes might result in her death, she vowed to be 'baptised in my own blood'. Despite having, with her husband, murdered her own daughter out of hatred for the faith, Manche's mother herself received baptism 41 years later in 1969. In 1998 a stone statue of Manche Masemola was placed above the Great West Door of Westminster Abbey in London alongside other 20th century Christian martyrs.

In Procession to the Burial Site of Manche Masemola

After four Christmases in South Africa, Hoey was summoned back to the mother house at Mirfield to be Prior. Reflecting on his inner life he explains:

I went because vowed to obedience. I felt I had been growing in the Mission work. I came to realise that obedience bears fruit. Though in some ways I felt quite useless, nevertheless I felt I was growing within myself. When I was made Prior, on the face of it a crazy decision, I didn't feel competent . I was younger than the other three, did not have the language and had to learn to say mass phonetically. I had to hear Confessions with a list of sins in English and the help of a subdeacon who communicated the penitents' confession by a system with bells. But the Africans didn't seem to mind.

Because there was little I could do, I could actually spend more time praying. I learned a lot about community living. Parishioners were killed by lightning every year. Walls lit up with blue light as lightning hit the conductors. I felt totally helpless before nature. There were creepy-crawlies everywhere. Water was a precious commodity with one bath per week. I grew fond of the African people. But I was delighted to be summoned home.

Hoey returned to Europe by air, stopping overnight in Rome on the way to visit his sister briefly in Malta. The renowned Archbishop Gonzi, whom his sister knew, had just written a Pastoral Letter against Prime Minister Don Mintoff. Hoey met the Archbishop at a lunch party at his sister's home. From Malta, he returned to Mirfield in time for Easter, 1961, where he had been summoned because he was *needed to get the place in order.*

chapter 6

Mirfield, London, Mirfield

FR AUGUSTINE HAD BEEN SUMMONED BACK from Africa to Mirfield by the Superior, Fr Jonathan Graham CR, to serve as Prior. He had been nominated in the General Chapter, of January 1961 and was elected by the July General Chapter. Hoey spent the first year 'at home' in Mirfield. He saw the Head of each 'Department' weekly to check up on the range of activities necessary to keep a religious house operating. An early innovation was the Introduction of cleaning ladies because he found that *the place was filthy*. He had been stirred into action by the state of a gentleman's urinal, which was particularly offensive; but *dust was everywhere* — the gesture of Hoey's brethren of the finger drawn along surfaces comes to mind again.

At this time in the community there were over 20 novices. *The place was full* — *it was hard to find enough beds for Chapter with the number of brethren attending*. The community at that time numbered eight houses, including those in South Africa and in Barbados, where CR ran Codrington Theological College, training men for the Anglican priesthood.

After the initial year, Hoey undertook some travel, including a visit to the house in Barbados. He preached Holy Week at St George's, Paris in 1963, staying with the Countess De Brosses who noted that he made the effort to speak a little French and amazed the neighbours by appearing in forms of clerical dress long since disappeared from view. Her husband had asked, "why does he have to stay here?" but was soon won over; they found Hoey a very good house guest who, she was delighted to discover, had a good sense of humour and enjoyed a glass of wine. Her husband was Catholic and she recalls that Hoey told her she should become a Roman Catholic too.

He also undertook further Missions, including a tour in the United States, where a number of parishes had connections with Mirfield, including Saint Clement's, Philadelphia, where he came under pressure to accept an invitation to become parish priest. While he was on the tour, news came of the death of Jonathan Graham, leaving Hoey as Prior without a Superior.

In the General Chapter at Mirfield in July 1966, Hoey was appointed Prior of the Community's house in West London at Holland Park. These paragraphs from a letter from Hoey to a friend, reflect on the impending move:

11.11.66

I am to be installed as Prior of London on the 25ᵗʰ of this month. We have long felt that CR wanted an entirely 'new look' in London, so I am to go and try to bring it off. I am more than delighted to be in London and to get rid of the dreary administrative tasks here...

I was very ill from Jan–June, due mainly to overwork. The stresses and strains sent my waterworks all wrong & I was in hospital for several weeks. But all that is behind me now and I feel better than for several years.

Saint Paul's Priory was located at 8, Holland Park, W11, to the West of Kensington Gardens. There was a chapel with furnishings by Martin Travers. Hoey recalls that the rest of the house *was filthy and furnished with odds and ends* and one senses that Hoey saw no future in the place, which was closed on 13 June, 1968. It was sold to become the Russian Embassy (and has subsequently been renovated as an upmarket apartment).

Saint Paul's Priory, Holland Park

Hoey inherited a tradition of Sales of Work at the St Ermine's Hotel near St James's Park station, to raise money for CR's school at Penhalonga in South Africa. He rapidly abandoned them as young people would not come. Instead he introduced the 'Africa Balls' held at Kensington Town Hall and at the Porchester Hall, Chelsea. Three were held, *run by a committee including wealthy people. I tried to get people with titles for the Committee. We also had 'celebrities'. Dora Bryan (a well-known TV actress) sat on it twice. Derek Nimmo (an actor also known for playing clergymen on TV) was the Patron and came, talking about CR's work in Africa.* These were expensive occasions to run and to attend, but were effective in their purpose of raising funds.

Beyond the life of the Priory, Fr Christopher Jackson recalls how he heard Hoey preach at the University Church in London.

I cannot recall what he said on that occasion except that it was powerful and challenged me, and others, to consider how serious we really were in our discipleship. Indeed, *challenging* is the word I would use to describe Augustine's ministry; his preaching was accessible to everyone but uncompromising, never banal. At the same time one sensed that in spite of failures to live up to what he proposed he would never wash his hands of you. I found this to be especially true when he preached a retreat for priests at Walsingham around 1972 and I went to him for the Sacrament of Reconciliation.

Hoey was planning a move which would take CR to the Royal Foundation of Saint Katharine in the East End of London. The Royal Foundation was founded in 1147 by Queen Matilda, the wife of King Stephen (not to be confused with his cousin and rival of the same name). She placed it in the custody of the Priory of the Holy Trinity at Aldgate, saying that they were to "maintain in the said Hospital in perpetuity 13 poor persons for the salvation of the soul of my lord, King Stephen and of mine, and also for the salvation of our sons, Eustace and William and of all our children". The duties of the Foundation lay in celebrating Mass, especially for the souls of those mentioned in the Charter, and in serving the poor infirm people in the Hospital. Matilda obtained a site on the east side of the Tower of London and a Church and Hospital were built there among open fields beside the river. After two centuries of disagreements and uncertainty, in 1351 Queen Philippa, the wife of Edward III, drew up new regulations, giving sisters equal rights with their male colleagues. The Foundation made its way through the vicissitudes of the Reformation but by the nineteenth century it had become little but a grace-and-favour residence. It was not until 1914 during the First World War, that St Katharine's funds were put to more appropriate use. Some of the funds were transferred to the Royal College of St Katharine, which was set up by Queen Alexandra, the widow of Edward VII, to undertake welfare work in Poplar.

Hoey with Queen Elizabeth, the Queen Mother, at St Katharine's

In July 1968, General Chapter appointed Hoey to be Prior of St Katharine's. The Royal Foundation's website comments that "in 1969 St Katharine's once more passed into the care of a religious order. The Patron, Queen Elizabeth the Queen Mother, entrusted it to the Community of the Resurrection, an Anglican order whose mother house was at Mirfield in the West Riding of Yorkshire. The Community supplied priests as Brethren and they were joined by the Deaconess Community of St Andrew who provided Sisters, so that St Katharine's was once more staffed by men and women religious, living in its old district, combining regular prayer and worship with ministering to the people of the surrounding area and providing a place of counsel, sanctuary and refuge to those in difficulty. The Foundation's educational functions continued with conferences on many issues facing Christians in the modern world."

Hoey initially lived there alone with the other brethren camping out in nearby Vicarages. In due course the Fathers regrouped at St Katharine's with members of the Deaconess Community of Saint Andrew. The participants felt that the Foundation had thus reverted to what it had originally been. During a stay of four months on the way from Mirfield to South Africa, Fr Crispin Harrison CR recalls:

> ...brick dust from the renovation works. The lower rooms in the main house had sea paintings by an Italian and an English artist, with blues and browns prevailing. Colourful fabrics were chosen

by Mrs Kirwan-Taylor of Eaton Square and Sussex, while Mary Hunter used to bring a crate of Bells whisky.

Hoey focused on the Mastership, apart from visits to the Community of the Holy Rood, Middlesbrough, of which he was Warden, and did not lead Missions during this period. The Africa Balls relocated to Bethnal Green Town Hall.

Back in Mirfield there was some uncertainty when the Community began the process to elect a new Superior. Augustine had been proposed for the role and Hugh Bishop was standing for a second term. In the first ballot neither Hoey nor Bishop had sufficient votes, but on Saturday 28th December 1968 Hugh Bishop was re-elected as Superior by General Chapter. Hoey comments *I think I was relieved — in a community there is no way to get rid of problem people.*

Reflecting on Hoey's London period, Stephen Lambert, who had known Hoey since childhood, writes as follows:

My earliest recollection of him was on one of his many visits to South Park, where I was brought up. I was four years old and Augustine, then a Mirfield Father, came to my room to say bedtime prayers with me. The memory has never left me; the aura of wordless prayer that hovers around him, that even reached out and left an indelible mark on the consciousness of a very young child.

My parents were in continual contact with CR. Father Raynes, for many years the Superior, introduced many people to the Faith at the twice yearly 'Holy Parties' held at South Park, which started in 1949 and continued until long after his death in 1958. (These were essentially residential 'country house' week-ends at my parents' home, where Fr Raynes and his successors gave talks; — 'gin and religion'!) Augustine was one of the Mirfield Fathers who came regularly to stay with us, often to have a few days of rest after one of his Parish Missions. As I grew up, I never lost contact with him.

In 1967, Augustine was Prior of the London House of CR — at that time in Holland Park. My parents thought it wise to base me there during the week whilst I was doing a sixth month course in London, rather than leaving the 18 year old to make his own arrangements! It was for me an introduction to the Religious Life. On many days I was able to attend all the Offices as well as Mass. I ate with the Community, sharing the fast days and feast days (coffee for breakfast on major Saints' Days!). I became very aware of Augustine's mission work in parishes up and down the country, helping priests to deepen and broaden the outreach of the Church in towns and cities.

In the late 1960's CR moved their London house to the Royal Foundation of St Katharine (Dockland) and Augustine was Master. Under his command the observance of The Triduum and Celebration of Easter Day was a very moving experience. A good friend of mine, an atheist originally, whose spiritual journey blossomed into priesthood, was prepared for confirmation at St Katharine's, and first experienced the ceremonies of Holy Week kept properly there. He writes "(I was) wide eyed with wonder at a liturgy that seemed as exotic as anything out of the Arabian Nights — the washing of feet (everybody's feet) on Maundy Thursday with a little kiss on each one's foot after it had been dried), the Watch at the Altar of Repose which in those days was kept through until the start of the Good Friday liturgy.... the silent Meditation on Good Friday, the liturgy of the burial in the garden... and the lighting of the New Fire in a great dustbin in the very early hours of Sunday morning with the sky turning gradually from black to grey to daylight during the Vigil — all nine readings in full with nothing at all omitted". I too had spent the Triduum at St Katharine's and knew well how Augustine's sense of theatre and quality of presentation of the liturgy is able to open out even the most clam-like of souls to the grace and love of the Holy Trinity.

Apart from the Liturgical and spiritual life at Saint Katharine's, Hoey offered the use of the Royal Foundation's facilities for gay people to meet socially. The Sexual Offences Act of 1967 had decriminalised homosexual acts in private between two men, both of whom had attained the age of 21. The Revd Dr Malcolm Johnson, then Anglican Chaplain at Queen Mary College, University of London and who in 1976 was one of the founders of the Gay Christian Movement, wrote about this in his diary:

> 26-28 July 1968. I have offered to do counselling for the Albany Trust so attend their conference at Wychcroft in Surrey and meet 30 of its supporters some of whom I know already such as Dr Hugh Pettiford, Ken Plummer and Peter Rose. The question put to us is 'What should the Trust do now that the Sexual Offences

Act was passed last year?' We agreed that more law reform is needed as it is difficult to give help to a teenager, and that the age of consent should come down from 21 to 18. I was particularly concerned at the lack of decent places for gays to meet, so Andrew Henderson, Christopher Spence and I agreed to set up a social group at the Royal Foundation of St Katharine in Stepney. Fr Augustine Hoey, its Master, was present and offered their Hall. It is a courageous offer and I gather that the Boss there (the Queen Mum) has agreed.

Shortly after this conference Johnson asked Hoey to be his spiritual director and recalls that

he was a very direct director and one needed to stand up to him! He was wise, liberal and supportive…

The SK Group met every Saturday evening in the common room and then as numbers increased we moved to the school hall. To begin with we wondered if the police would raid the group but we were a respectable group backed by a royal foundation. It was the first non commercial gay social group. Augustine wearing his black Mirfield cassock would usually spend an hour with us and members, who included a number of clergy, got to know him and probably asked to see him for counselling. The SK group closed around 1995.

I remember he would say 'How are you?' Then after pleasantries 'How are you **really**?' He is one of the few true celibates I have met. He usually came to our gay parties and once I naughtily introduced him to a handsome man who fancied him and made it plain. Augustine said thank you but no thank you!

Hoey (second from right) with Michael Ramsey (Archbishop of Canterbury) and Reverend Mother OHP at Whitby

He always looked so smart and trim and Aramis toilet water, supplied by friends, was liberally used. He asked me to speak at various weekend courses he arranged at the Foundation. Unlike today St Katharine's held many retreats and conferences and Augustine organised one on 'Ways of loving' — married, gay, monks and nuns etc and the old ladies asked me searching questions!

I became Master of the Royal Foundation in 1992 and Augustine was a tremendous help in my planning the future of the Foundation. When I saw him over a year ago he told me that the Queen Mum said that the SK Group was 'very necessary'.

During the period at Saint Katharine's, Hoey felt more and more drawn to a life of prayer. In this letter, he explains to a friend: *I have waited so long for it and in spite of being a bit scared that at last it has happened, nothing shakes the deep inner conviction.*

22.1.72

I am giving up the Mastership of St Katharine's in July and returning to Mirfield in order to be able to experiment with a life more totally structured to prayer and silence. There is a long history behind this, because for many years I have felt the growing conviction that for me the only way in which I could fulfil my urge 'to love and care' for all mankind is through direct prayer. In every kind of pastoral and evangelistic situation one is limited by physical conditions to the particular individual or group one is in dialogue with at the time. I always feel I want to go beyond this, to be able to embrace all humanity at once, to be used 'to bring light to them that sit in the shadow of death' — and there is no other way except through prayer and in particular the prayer of intercession. Moreover the confusion of the age in which we live only quickens my feeling that this is the way in which I can help best. This involves a greater withdrawal, more silence and less physical involvement than is possible in any of the branch houses of CR.

It was 12 years ago when I was Prior of our house in Sekhukuniland that I first asked the chapter of my community for permission to live the life of prayer. It was not granted — because both then and on subsequent occasions when I have made the same request — it did not seems possible for me to be released from the particular work the community had committed to me at the time. However at our recent January Chapter it was unanimously decided that I should withdraw from St Katharine's and do a year's experimental period at the mother house of putting into practice the 'vision' which has pursued me for so long. I hope to begin this on July 25, St James's Day, which is the anniversary of my Profession. I may of course be making a great mistake and chasing some projected fantasy of my own dramatic imagination — but the 12 months will be a means of discovering both for me and my community whether the desire is of God or of men.

I do not feel I am escaping anything, but rather expanding and enlarging my horizons and you will still be in my heart as I pray. Please remember me too, for there are bound to be moments when the withdrawal will seem to be both empty and meaningless.

So it was that Hoey returned to Mirfield to live in community, but with a distinctive routine of prayer suited to his sense of vocation. General Chapter in July 1972 confirmed his move from London to the Mother House by noting a change of Residence. Hoey went daily to the Community Church for Morning Prayer at 3 a.m. at the start of his celebration of the sevenfold office, joining the Community for the Midday Office and Evening Prayer. He lived more or less in silence, his inner 'desert' life focusing on intercession.

Chapel, Royal Foundation of St Katharine, rebuilt in 1952 on the site of the original chapel

A few months after his move back to Mirfield, reflecting on the period Hoey wrote:

As I look back through the years from this November of 1972 I know full well that only the thought of union with the Passion has seen me through so many difficult, despairing, lonely, dark and threatening situations. The Agony in Gethsemane has pushed me on when my whole being shrank back in fear to say 'no'. It has helped me enormously so to be able to find God in the very heart of the frustration, darkness and bewilderment.

It seems to me that at the moment throughout Christendom there is a falling away from the emphasis on the Cross; yet how can we experience resurrection without it? It is the fashion of the day to find an anaesthetic for everything, or to try to. Psychiatry and drugs have their place in severe forms of stress and mental illness, but often they are only palliative. Sooner [or later] all Christians who wish to deepen their personal relationship with God must taste the dereliction of Christ and find in every aspect of the Passion a type of the many divisive situations in which mankind finds himself strangled today.

The title of a book by Carlo Carretto, "The Desert in the City" reflected that a contemporary movement of spirituality and circumstances were developing that led to the next decisive step in Hoey's life. He was hoping to get a flat in Hulme and to live his desert life in the city of Manchester.

chapter 7

Emmaus in Manchester and Sunderland

I N AUGUST 1973, Hoey went to visit a parish in Hulme, Manchester where the curate, the Revd Graeme Oakes, had Mirfield connections. There was a complex of new flats. Violence, crime and prostitution were rife — Hoey felt it was just *the place for a House of Prayer*. A flat was made available, the Community agreed and at the end of August 1973 a majority of CR brethren endorsed Augustine's request and the project formally began. The first Emmaus was born at 542 John Nash Crescent, M15 5DS.

Hoey seems to have begun his time in Manchester with at least outward calm, but this was not necessarily shared by his neighbours in Hulme.

> *People were bewildered at first. They thought I had been sent to reform prostitution. In the end I loved it. I felt I was living with real people who didn't pretend. On one side my neighbours were professional thieves — they stole during the day and then sold goods on at night. On the other side lived a faded, African prostitute. Nearby lived another woman with seven children, each with a different father, who came back each night with different men. The life of prayer released some kind of force for good to cancel the darkness all around. I wanted to draw people to prayer. The flats are well planned inside, but material planning, however well thought out, does not change people. We are equally divided between wild Irish, West Indians and the people of Manchester's former slums.*

Among the practical help offered by the neighbours was a suggestion from the people next door that Emmaus should be re-wired so that the electricity used would not pass through the meter. Hoey politely declined!

At Emmaus, Hulme the same routine was kept as during Hoey's contemplative period at Mirfield, with the sevenfold office and intercessory prayer commencing at 3.00 a.m. One hour of silent prayer was observed in the morning and another in the evening.

Hoey felt he *was doing more for the people by prayer than by preaching missions. In the early days I would say that I put up with living alone. Each day was lived with an intention. Total silence was observed all day, broken only at coffee. My mind was on the intention all the time — work was part of the offering.*

The Community sent different members to stay at weekends, so Hoey was not entirely alone. In due course, Fr Alexander Cox CR moved to live at Emmaus.

The following account of Hoey's time at Emmaus, Hulme, from the Revd Graham Weir, speaks for itself:

> If you don't know already, it's very important to try and grasp at the outset something of Hulme, Manchester and what it was like during Augustine's time there.
>
> Hulme had gone through a massive 1960s slum clearance. During this time most of the old Hulme people had been moved out to areas of Greater Manchester like Fallowfield, Sale, Withington, Wythinshaw and Hattersley Hyne. Some were even moved as far as Glossop. The old Hulme housing stock was absolutely decimated and the community had its heart ripped out and its people were dispersed throughout the Mancunian conurbations.
>
> The area had been rebuilt with concrete "Bull Ring" crescent blocks each housing hundreds of families. Most of the people who were moved back into the area were not from Hulme and most had their own social, economic and medical stories to tell. It seemed that every needy person from the Greater Manchester area found their way to Hulme.
>
> With this influx of outsiders came every kind of social, economic and communitarian problem known to man. Unemployment, the poor concrete housing arrangements and the sheer number of people living on top of each other ensured that Hulme grew into a "problem" area. Parts of the area became very much a law unto themselves.
>
> The law of the street prevailed and even those of us who were brought up and lived there also had to be very careful where we went and with whom we associated.
>
> During the sixties, Church life had grown irrelevant to many of the teenagers of Hulme. We dreamed of becoming footballers or joining rock bands in order to escape the poverty. In the late sixties I did escape Hulme and joined the British Army. Ill-

disciplined and poorly educated as I was, the Army seemed to offer a worthwhile escape and many of my friends took similar opportunities, though a number weren't what you might call voluntary and served time in various borstals. By 1969 the furthest I'd ever travelled till I joined the army was Blackpool. And the British Army posters and billboards promised worldwide travel and a career. In what, we weren't quite sure.

The 'bullrings' in Hulme where Emmaus was first established

After trips to Scotland, Northumberland, Germany, Cyprus and two tours in Northern Ireland with the Parachute Regiment, I returned to Hulme. I was now very out of touch with life on the streets of Hulme. Compared with many of my previous contemporaries my self-discipline and education had improved significantly, I had travelled and wanted to put something back into the community. I did a very strange thing and returned to Church. This absolutely 'gobsmacked' my family now living out in Fallowfield and my girlfriend at the time. But I got a job helping to supervise local Hulme/Moss side kids on the adventure playgrounds in the area. I was surprised but absolutely delighted to find that my old vicar Revd Gordon Dowden had remained in Hulme after the slum clearance and the building of the "Bull Rings". He had supervised the transition of building a new Church in the wake of the demolition of our old Parish Church of St Philip. The new Church was built right in the heart of the "Bull Rings" — The Church of the Ascension, Hulme.

Apart from the local Clergy from the various denominations I quickly discovered that no other "Professional" people lived in Hulme. The local GPs, Social workers, School Teachers and those who worked in the library, even the local shop owners lived outside of Hulme in the more leafy suburbs. And who could blame them?

I became aware that a Priest in a cassock began attending our Sunday morning services at the Ascension and would occasionally take the service particularly on weekdays. He also did his shopping in our local shops. We also had a new young Curate, the Revd Geoffrey Morgan. Though we were from very different backgrounds he and I became quite good friends. He told us that this strange chap was some sort of monk and was living in the "Bull Rings".

Of course the local criminal fraternity got wind of him and it wasn't long before they were trying to sell him the odd TV or two. Lots of other interesting types also found their way to his door. I think I'm correct in saying that Augustine's flat was never broken into during his time in Hulme. If that's true than believe me, his was the only one.

I'd become an active member of the Ascension and became a very regular communicant on Sundays and through the week. Eventually I attended a short Lent course on prayer. To my surprise this chap in the black cassock was leading it. He was introduced as Fr Augustine Hoey and we were told that he was living in one of the flats in the "Bull Rings" across from the Church.

What kind of a name was that, I thought? What's a posh git like him doing in Hulme? We have enough "do-gooders" — the place was aflood with Social Workers, Play leaders and Youth workers (usually rich university types) and a fat lot of difference they were making. We had our own Clergy so why did we need more and; more to the point, why would some crank choose to come and live here? All our energy was focused on getting out of the place.

Of course many of us across the Adventure Playground community were full of the idealistic dreams of making Hulme a better place for everyone. But it was an uphill battle against growing crime, drugs, gangs and all the social economic problems these activities bring. Thankfully, the gun culture which eventually made Hulme/Moss side nationally famous had not then begun to surface.

The Youth of the area were well out of control and extremely streetwise as they always had been. They had nowhere to go and the churches and social agencies were valiantly fighting a rear guard action by trying to provide a focus for community living and Christian discipleship.

The course on prayer I remember. Well what I really remember is the sentence Augustine used from Psalm 46 v 10: "Be still and know that I am God". Over the coming year or so I slowly got to know Augustine. When I eventually visited his flat in the "Bull Ring" I was blown away. At first I classically attacked what I didn't understand and what disturbed me. I had never heard the word 'monk' before, let alone shared coffee with one. We'd talk about prayer and I shared my experiences with him. He was inviting, engaging and very patient. Never once did I feel inadequate.

Over the months and years Augustine gently but firmly sat me down and shared with me something of the life he felt called by God to lead. A life of contemplative prayer in the heart of Hulme. Right there in the mess of it all this little offering for Hulme and the whole world.

I of course knew nothing then of the calling or value of such a ministry. Nor anything of the loving sacrifice such a ministry required — the self discipline of living for God alone through a rule of life. Nor anything of the riches and joy such a way of life could bring.

To the surprise of many I began to read both the Bible and, yes, even books. I eventually stumbled across a chap called St Francis of Assisi, who like me had been a soldier who, too, became disillusioned and was desperately love sick for something better and meaningful. The more I read the Gospels and the life of Francis the more Augustine got an ear bashing. But he patiently listened, watched and waited.

"What an absolute waste of time pottering around saying prayers all the time in a block of flats, when the Church and the people were falling apart around our ears. Why doesn't he (notice I never said WE) get out and DO something. Why can't the Church with all its wealth do something to help the poor? Sell its possessions and feed God's people?"

I can see Augustine now in my minds-eye. The little smile and chuckle. How his little disciple protesteth much, he must have thought. He no doubt saw where all this was heading and just gently guided me along.

Within a couple of years I had given away all that I possessed and left Hulme never to return, to join the Anglican Franciscan Order, the Society of St Francis. Augustine officially became my spiritual director and I valued greatly his council, though I can't say I always followed it. I have always been a disobedient disciple. However his prayerful attentiveness and disciplined life has for almost forty years been an eminent support to me and although we have never lived in each others pockets I have valued greatly his ministry of prayer and his ability just to be there.

And what of me now? Well I survived the Novitiate but withdrew towards the end of my third year. I married thirty-odd years ago, had two children and became a Priest in the Church of England. Some years ago I had a terrible shock whilst reading an article in a Religious Communities Magazine which implied that Augustine had died. After some frantic internet searching I discovered that the article was incorrect. Praise the Lord he hadn't died and I travelled down to London to celebrate by having lunch with him.

We still keep in touch. Though we are so very different on so many levels, we find ourselves spiritually united in Christ and interwoven into each others' prayer. He has been a constant prayerful companion to me through some very difficult times of illness. And I believe I have been very fortunate to have met him and to have been richly blessed through his devotion to God and his ministry of prayer.

Hoey's own views on the work of Emmaus emerge from a letter written to a friend:

30.3.75

About mid-December I developed acute bronchitis, was bundled into a car and driven to Mirfield, where I was put to bed for three weeks. I managed to stagger into choir for the last Mass of Christmas Day — then back to bed — and finally returned to Manchester, feeling rather wan, in Mid-January...

It was decided in our January 1975 Chapter to continue with Emmaus for another twelve months and then to reconsider the situation again. The community feels that the life of prayer as it is carried out at Emmaus will help the community to renew itself and to discover how best to serve the church and the world in this day and age. In future, the brethren will come to stay at Emmaus for longer periods than last year, in order to enter more deeply into the 'feel and style' of the life.

It is difficult to assess the last twelve months, for the effect of the life of prayer is beyond human calculation. There are some days of darkness and bewilderment, but others when in an undefinable way there is a sense of being near the heart of things. John Nash Crescent is part of the concrete jungle of Hulme, near the city centre of Manchester. The neighbours have accepted Emmaus as part of the scene, although I don't suppose they would be very articulate about its significance. Everyone is friendly and although they would not define Emmaus as

The chapel at Emmaus, Hulme

'a visible sign of the eternal', yet I am sure many 'sense' it as that. As I have probably told you before, violence, prostitution, drug addiction, marital confusion, debt, drunkenness and excessive gambling are the stuff of life in Hulme and a pathetic belief that money can buy happiness. In the midst of all this the recitation of the Psalms in the daily round of Offices is highlighted. The words are like the voice of Hulme, just because the Psalms vividly express every human mood, desire, groping, bewilderment and even cursing. They include the desire for vindication, the bitter complaint against injustice, the cry of the man crushed by hopelessness and frustration and feeling himself forsaken by God and wholly at the mercy of the forces of evil. The psalms also express joy and praise and delight in God, in human love and in creation... So in this work of prayer one is trying to be a bridge-builder between man and God.

Requests for prayer have continued to increase throughout the year and I am always glad to be able to weave these into the Office. I do this for one month and then stop unless directed otherwise. But it is even more important to be thankful for all God IS and the way in which he reveals Himself in our neighbour, in difficult circumstances and in situations which from a human point of view seem well nigh intractable. He is always there, if we have eyes to see and ears to listen. It is the joy of this truth which helps us to balance the burden of intercession which is so often concerned with the anguish and stress of mankind.

On 3 January 1974 The Superior of CR, Hugh Bishop resigned, to the shock of the Chapter, and left immediately. In this letter written three months later, Hoey commented:

The less said about Hugh Bishop the better. I am very traditional about these things and regard the whole episode as a great betrayal. You can imagine the effect on poor CR; it has left many in a sadly bewildered state. We have temporarily closed the novitiate and I think it will be some time before we get ourselves on an even keel again and will probably have to experience more 'dying' first.

There is nothing much I can report about life in Manchester except that it just goes on. The life is not always easy — days of backward glances, days of thinking what I might be doing instead and days when the future seems totally obscure. Yet, deep down, there is the underlying conviction of being on 'the right path' and I suppose it is inevitable, if one is drawn to intercession, one is sticking one's neck out to experience something of the dereliction and meaninglessness of life that haunts mankind.

I have fought many 'demons' since I took up residence in the concrete wilderness and the initial stages I would not like to repeat, but underneath the bewilderment and the questions which often haunt me, is the deep-rooted conviction that I am on the right 'way'. I don't know what the neighbours make of it all, but they are all friendly and helpful (especially the children) as I go about the daily business of shopping, the launderette etc.

With the arrival back at Mirfield of Fr Maurice Bradshaw, CR from South Africa, who wanted to be at Emmaus, the Manchester house was too small. Augustine addressed the July General Chapter, 1976 on the matter which gave its permission for the renting of St John's Vicarage, Sunderland. Emmaus was to continue, but in the North-East.

Canon Michael Whitehead recalls the early stages of planning for the new Emmaus:

Augustine wrote round to various friends asking if we knew of a house which would be suitable. I wrote almost by return to tell him of the former St John's Vicarage in the East End of Sunderland and in our parish. The house, though basically sound, was in a poor state of repair and a cause of worry to us. Part of it was occupied by the redoubtable Mary Hedley, a retired moral welfare worker employed by Durham Diocese. She had done sterling work in South Shields...

Augustine was immediately attracted to St John's Vicarage as he had known Sunderland from his teenage years — Philip Strong who was Vicar of St Ignatius in the 1930s had been his parish priest at Christ Church, Meadow Lane, Leeds. Augustine had joined the Wooler Camps in the Cheviots organised by Algy Robertson who was a curate of St George's Cullercoats, with Philip Strong and other priests and religious. And I expect he had met Canon Jackson who was then Vicar of St John's and lived in the house.

Augustine replied at once and came and we looked over the place. CR gave permission for Emmaus to move there and Augustine closed the flat in Hulme and came to live in the Clergy House at St Ignatius — the old one in Mowbray Road — for several months while he superintended the makeover of St John's Vicarage. As you would expect, no detail was too small for his close attention. He became well-known in the main stores in Sunderland and the only setback was the liquidation of the firm supplying and fitting the carpets. In the end the only loss was the free fitting because he was able to arrange the collection and storing of the carpets before the liquidators closed in.

A remarkable clearing and cleaning exercise by an army of volunteers from among the faithful rendered the old Vicarage spick and span in time for the small firm of local builders to renew the wiring and plumbing, fit washbasins in all the study bedrooms, and refit the bathrooms and kitchen.

Jean Hall was a parishioner of St Ignatius Sunderland and one of the lay people supporting the arrival and continuing work of the Brethren at Emmaus.

Fr Augustine came and lived with Fr Michael at St Ignatius' Clergy House while he had the job of preparing the house. In no time he had collected many people, with different skills and know-how. I worked for a mail-order firm and he was always coming to look at the Catalogue and bought most of the things to set up the bedrooms. There was joinery work — every bedroom had washbasins, with mirrors above and he saw to all of that. One of the rooms in the house became the Chapel — he always emphasised prayer. So he prayed very much about what was needed. One thing was a hanging Pyx for the Chapel. The Countess, a friend, provided it. At Emmaus, Sunday was an Open Day, and we were all invited to join them for a cup of tea around the table.

Canon Whitehead's account continues:

For the Chapel there was also a newly-created statue of Our Lady of Walsingham. Finally, when all was completed to Augustine's satisfaction, Alexander [Cox] and Maurice [Bradshaw] joined him and the new Emmaus was blessed and opened in 1977.

I have a vivid memory of driving to the House at Mirfield to collect Augustine with a cache of belongings and, with him in the passenger seat, setting off back to Sunderland.

At first, the brethren kept a full round of the Divine Office and daily Mass. This included a night Vigil but this was modified later. Almost at once clergy and laity made use of the facilities for Quiet Days, Retreats and Spiritual Direction.

Augustine shopped locally and in that remarkable way of his soon drew many of the people living in 'The Garths' and in the

The former Vicarage of St John's Sunderland where Emmaus was established in 1977

Trafalgar Square Almshouses into a close relationship.

The Fathers and guests worshipped in Holy Trinity, the old Sunderland Parish Church, and in St Ignatius' up the road on

Sundays and Solemnities. The clergy of the parish, members of the Company of Mission Priests, valued Emmaus and became good friends with the Fathers. This was true, too, of both congregations who were generous to the community. There were memorable Holy Weeks and characteristic Augustine Christmases (with several cribs in various parts of Emmaus).

The impact of Emmaus was profound — it underlines the importance and effectiveness of the Church 'being there'. Incarnational it certainly was. Three CMP priests and one layman subsequently became religious. I believe Emmaus affected their response to that call.

In a circular letter to local clergy, Augustine introduced the project:

Emmaus, Prospect Row,
Sunderland,
SR1 2BP, Tyne & Wear.

Dear

The Anglican Community of the Resurrection, Mirfield, has opened a house of prayer in the east-end of Sunderland under the name of Emmaus. It was blessed by the Bishop of Durham on June the eleventh. The house stands close by the river looking across to the site of the monastery where the Venerable Bede spent so many years of his earthly life. It is the first time in the eighty-five years of the Community of the Resurrection that this experiment is being made of establishing a house where the life is totally structured to the work of prayer. There are three members of the Community in permanent residence with others coming and going.

It is a house of silence and prayer for mankind where the suffering and doubt of humanity are heard very clearly and felt very deeply and where the things of this world are seen in a truer perspective and proportion, because they are seen in the light of God's purpose. We shall be glad to pray for anyone you wish. Write the full name and particulars on a card.

The prayer will be offered for one month and can be renewed on request.

The house is available for confessions and counselling. Please make an appointment. The house is open for those who wish to make quiet days or retreats - both men and women. Guests are welcome to stay, but they will be expected to take a full share in the life, including the night office on the days when it is said.

The Fathers will NOT be available for outside work except on Sunday mornings when they are free for preaching or celebrating the Eucharist if due notice is given. Transport must be provided both ways as we have no car and Sunday morning transport is so limited.

Please pray for us as we labour in prayer to bring the needs of Sunderland and the world before God.

Yours in Christ,

In addition to the expectation of attendance at the night office, visitors were also expected to assist with housework. Fr Crispin Harrison recalls a system of cards handed out, the one he received beginning, 'Kindly dust the stairs, including Our Lady's statue...'

Although most visitors to Emmaus were struck by the intensity of the life there, the tables were turned on Hoey when Rowan Williams, a teacher at the College of the Resurrection (and later Archbishop of Canterbury) came to stay for a couple of weeks while thinking about entering the religious life. Hoey was overwhelmed *by his terrible intensity. We got up to pray at 2.30 a.m. and in the morning decided to allow ourselves a boiled egg for breakfast. We were rebuked by Rowan Williams who said "this egg is an unnecessary luxury in which I should not be participating." But I did like him, though intensity flowed out of his pores.* Lord Williams himself recalls conversations with Hoey about the priesthood in which he sensed an approach typical of the older generation of Mirfield priests. He found something of the emotionally controlled approach of Fr Raymond Raynes, and hints of a bleak mixture of 'Anglican reticence, Sulpician priestly theology and a dash of Carmelite darkness'. But Hoey was unusual with his dramatic mission style and the hint of the theatrical impresario.

Hoey himself found complete continuity in the move to Sunderland. His intercessory prayer was offered against the background of the image of tower blocks which he described as *bleak, with layers of bodies, totally vulnerable. It was impossible to feel isolated. Endless guests came to visit — they had to share the life, including rising at 3 a.m.*

On April 8, 1978, at a Solemn Eucharist in All Saints', Margaret Street, London W1 celebrated by the Rt Revd Robert Runcie, Bishop of Saint Alban's, Hoey married his niece Philippa to Christopher Luckcraft. The couple had been present at the inauguration of Emmaus. He commented:

Everything was <u>marvellous</u>. Nothing went wrong. A few hours later at 3 a.m. I was admitted to the Westminster Hospital where I stayed for 3 weeks, had prostate gland surgery, followed by complications and a month's convalescence, divided between Worthing and the Lamberts at South Park.

Christopher Jackson, now a Catholic priest but then an Anglican Vicar, reflects:

Working then in nearby South Shields I asked Augustine to be my spiritual director and would go to Emmaus for a regular Day of Recollection. The chapel, and indeed the whole house, was simply furnished but with impeccable taste — an atmosphere of prayer and recollection that was palpable. Advice was given by Augustine on removals: *Never use (the name of a well-known firm). They moved us in here and the foreman came to me and said, "Very sorry Guv but we've knocked the 'ands off that doll (Our Lady of Walsingham). Never mind, a bit of Bostik and she'll be fine."* At this point, shock and horror.

John Habgood, Bishop of Durham at the blessing of Emmaus, Sunderland

A young man, William Nicol, who had recently moved to Sunderland, was greatly influenced by Hoey during this period:

I can say without reservation that no single individual has had the impact or the influence on my life of Fr Hoey. I first met Augustine in Sunderland. I had recently moved into the parish and was attending St Ignatius the Martyr, Hendon and Augustine was in the CR house, Emmaus.

I had come from a fairly middle of the road Anglican tradition so both St Ignatius and Fr Hoey were slightly alien to me. However we became great friends. It was through Augustine that I ended up testing my vocation at Mirfield where I remained for 17 years until I was received into the Roman Catholic Church.

Hoey has always been sensitive to a dimension of reality which goes beyond the present and the physical. In 1979, he wrote these notes following a Retreat at Walsingham when he stayed in the accommodation known as 'The College'. This tells, in his own words, a story which has circulated widely in Anglican circles.

NOTES AFTER MAKING MY RETREAT AT WALSINGHAM, OCTOBER 1979

The 'magic' of the Shrine is stronger than ever and overwhelming. I have found it spiritually exhausting, but it is the kind of exhaustion which one wants to increase as one meets wave upon wave of human aspiration and anguish, of hope and despair washing through the doors of the Holy House. I have never felt so much part of humanity.

I had planned to make my retreat with only the Bible and Dostoyevsky's 'The Idiot'. I began this way, but after the first day both of these seemed to be getting in the way and I could only sit in the Shrine and walk through the country lanes trying to enter into the fullness of Mary's 'yes' to God. It was a wordless searching and one which I wanted not just for myself but for

the whole human race. It was a confrontation with both light and darkness, highlighted by my own personal questioning as to whether the Emmaus 'way' is the one God intends for me. Perhaps I was looking for a clear sign which would make the decision crystal clear

The chapel of Emmaus, Sunderland

and naturally the sign was not given! God does not often work this way. Just as Our Lady's 'yes' was a complete risk and entrance into the unknown, so I can't expect it to be any different for me. I left W with great regret, the question — Emmaus — to be or not to be — hanging in the air.

I found myself in a haunted room; at least haunted for me although Fr Careful, the Administrator, said it was the first time anyone had said anything about that particular room. The room, and those adjoining it, were all part of what had once been a row of very ancient cottages. I was on the first floor.

It was on the second night of the retreat when I suddenly awoke — wide awake — at 0400 hrs. The wall of bookshelves facing the bed had gone and in its place was a staircase coming up into the room. The first thing that took my eye was the floor round the top of the stairs. It was covered with very highly polished tiles. Half way down the stairs a man was standing looking at me. I could see him only from the waist upwards. He was wearing a brimmed soft flat hat of black velvet on a head of straight 'bobbed' dark hair. His face (which I can't really describe, although I would recognise it again) registered neither sorrow, distress nor joy... it was completely expressionless and he kept on looking at me. I felt no fear or alarm, no sense of evil or distaste. For a moment I was non-plussed and then I raised my right hand and, making the sign of the Cross said, 'May the Lord give you his peace.' Slowly he shook his head from side to side, again registering no kind of emotion. As I looked, the wall of bookshelves came back into focus and the 'seeing' disappeared. I looked at my clock. It was 0400 hrs.

It was not a bad haunting, but it was not a reassuring one either. I did not feel any kind of exorcism was required.

Would I be happy to sleep in the room again? I'm not sure. The 'man' kept his distance and I would not like the idea of his being nearer the bed. As I write this my legs and body are seized by unusual trembling. I would prefer not to sleep in the room again! When I told the 'administrator my experience of the 'ghost' in my bedroom he searched out the plan of the cottages which had stood on the site... he found there had once been a staircase where I saw it.

I have never cared to walk alone on the back lane from the Shrine to the parish church. It goes through what must formerly have been the Abbey Grounds and has a reputation for being haunted. It is a most beautiful country lane... I have never 'seen' anything, but there is one part near a ruined wall or gate of the old Abbey where I sense a sudden drop in temperature. Even on the warmest days with the sun shining in full blaze my body grows quite cold for about 10 yards and I grow disquieted within. I had this experience on the two occasions I walked along it during my retreat.

Though much appreciated by others, the life at Emmaus was leaving Hoey under increasing stress.

I wasn't very well — I had become totally exhausted. The doctor, Cardinal Hume's brother, thought I should have a rest. There had been increasing pestering from outside that I ought to be coming back and handing on the fruits. A hermit sister of Wantage (an Anglican religious community for women) wrote to me that the eremitical life is only for a time, there is the need to recharge.

Canon Whitehead closes the story:

When Augustine found he was unable to continue he was succeeded by Fr Aelred Stubbs CR who though quite different to Augustine was successful in leading Emmaus until it closed when numbers in the Community declined."

Fr Eric Simmons had become Superior of CR in 1974 and had supported the Emmaus project in Chapter, seeking to allay the doubts of some brethren who resisted what they felt was a slight 'self-dramatisation' on the part of Augustine. Simmons supported the move to Sunderland as a practical response for the need for more space, and enjoyed visiting the house. His view of Augustine was that although he could seem fussy, he was easy to get on with. There was a clear sense of discipline at Emmaus, and 'people knew what they were taking on'. Simmons remembers being cross when Augustine, at the start of his period of ill-health, said he thought he should go back to an apostolic life. He valued the whole project greatly and feared that it might collapse. Simmons recalls that when Hoey asked him, why are you cross with me, Superior? 'I could have hit him'.

The General Chapter of July, 1980 approved a change of residence for Augustine from Sunderland to the Mother House. He was appointed Sacristan, with Fr Clifford Green as Assistant Sacristan.

Hoey's return to Mirfield brought great excitement to the students training for ordination at the College of the Resurrection. Fr Kevin Robinson, then an ordinand at Mirfield and now a Catholic priest, captures the moment:

I remember seeing Augustine Hoey for the first time when I was a student at the College of the Resurrection. He appeared in the sanctuary of the great CR Church at Mirfield sometime in the early part of 1981. Newly appointed as sacristan, he seemed to glide effortlessly wherever he went as if there were hidden wheels beneath his cassock. The lights and books and vestments were all meticulously prepared and attended to. In winter he wore a unique over garment covering him from head to floor in shimmering black quilted insulation. It was probably the lining of an old long coat adapted for sacred duties.

Another aspect of Hoey's appearance that caused wonder among the College students was his uncreased scapular.

Back at Mirfield, Hoey had *no regrets and no disorientation. I prayed more than CR expected.* He did not enjoy being Sacristan (a fact that would have hugely surprised his student admirers) but cleaned the sacristy up — and was *relieved not to have to work in the kitchen.*

During this period, the programme of Missions resumed, each with a large team and following the classic Hoey pattern. One married couple, Susan and Richard Adams, took

The staircase with statue of Our Lady, Emmaus, Sunderland

part in five such Missions spanning a seven year period: Christchurch, Carnforth in 1984; St Aidan and St Columba, Hartlepool in 1987; Holy Trinity, Rothwell in autumn 1988; St Martin's, Torquay in 1990; and St Margaret's and St Andrew's Uxbridge in 1991.

At the General Chapter in July, 1983 Augustine was appointed Assistant House Steward at Mirfield. The next move came in 1984; Simmons was looking for someone to go to the Royal Foundation of Saint Katharine, Hoey offered — *If you want to send me, I'll go.* Simmons recalls that Hoey returned very gracefully, even though he was no longer in charge of the House he had set up in 1968.

chapter 8

London and Rome

A T THE ROYAL FOUNDATION of Saint Katharine the second time
round, Hoey collected penitents almost every day and handed
many on to other priests. Many were adults making their confession
for the first time. Among those who came to see him in London, some
were from smart wealthy families — *but I never sought them out*. He did
not go away much but conducted retreats and led some Missions.

Fr Christopher Jackson invited Hoey to lead a parish mission at St
Helen's, Hemsworth, a mining village in West Yorkshire:

> They were the most exhausting two weeks of my life and yet two
> of the most exhilarating. Once he had agreed to come I received
> many instructions about what was to be done, and when and how.
> A full-scale military operation with a General who knows exactly
> what he expects from his troops is the best way to describe it. The
> team was large — priests, laity, religious, theological students. I
> think that when he was getting a team together Augustine used
> to call in favours as everyone seemed to know him and no-one felt
> that they could do anything other than acquiesce. This became
> apparent at the early morning meetings when he would tell us
> what was to happen during the day and what everyone should
> be doing. He would then do the democratic thing and ask each
> person in turn if they had any questions. 'No, Father' was the usual
> response and people would then be out visiting, lunching with
> parishioners, and practising their part in the evening mission
> service until they met again for high tea. Augustine set a great deal
> of store on visiting and it paid off; people began to come to the
> mission services because they had been visited and were curious
> to find out what was going on. I love the story of Augustine
> discovering an elderly nun who was part of the team sitting in
> church one afternoon.
>
> "Sister, shouldn't you be out visiting?"
> "Oh yes Father, but I'm too tired."
> "Too tired, Sister...for Him?"

Whereupon Sister scuttled away to be about her Father's business. Apocryphal as this may be, it certainly captures the mood of a Hoey mission from the team's point of view.

Parishioners, and those who attended during the mission, saw the finished product which was always professional to a high degree: excellent catechesis including Augustine's addresses which I can only describe as mesmerising — a real attempt to answer the questions people will always ask about life and faith; an appeal to the heart. Following community hymn singing he would suddenly appear out of the darkness and stand, without notes, in a spotlight. When he spoke he could hold people's attention for as long as he wished. The success of the mission also depended on outdoor witness: processions round the streets with *tableaux vivantes* on the back of a truck;

Anglican National Pilgrimage to Walsingham, 1988

helium-filled balloons with details of the mission printed on them were distributed to children. After the evening service the team members would be found in one of the local clubs and Augustine would get up and tell people there about the mission. In one club some youths greeted this with derision and were roundly told off by their mates who apologised to Augustine on their behalf for 'showing us up.' I think that by that stage of his ministry Father had (reluctantly) agreed to one day off for the team at the mid-point of the mission but I cannot recall what we did — slept probably. I do remember that there was a free night when some of us wanted to go out of the parish for a drink but were sternly reminded that this might be the one night when someone who really wanted to speak to us in one of the local hostelries. It was the only parish event I can ever recall where numbers increased steadily throughout the week and people actually queued to get into church — rather like going to the cinema in the 1950s.

Clouds were gathering in the C of E however, and after the mission he wrote to tell me that on its final day he had received news of three more priests who had decided to leave and become Catholics: *It was a good thing that the spotlight could not show the sadness in my heart; what can one do or say?*

Fr Kevin Robinson writes about another aspect of Hoey's work in the 1980s:

As a student and Anglican seminarian I was already identified as having "Roman" tendencies. Early in 1982 the head of pastoral studies (Jack — later Bishop — Nichols) suggested that I might go to Augustine for a Confessor and Spiritual Director. Thereafter he has remained my confessor, stabiliser, spiritual director, soul friend, ecclesiastical MOT specialist, and some would add, fatal influence.

In 1982, Augustine had already served a lifetime with Roman tendencies, not only as a priest of the Church of England but as a devoted and faithful member of CR and a great parish missionary. It was felt that Augustine might help to give me stability to serve as a priest of the C of E in the same way. I remember going to him for the first time privately. After a long and patient conversation (the first of many over the next 34 years) he exclaimed: *When are you going to be ordained?* — "In June Father." — *Oh my goodness we have a lot of work to do!* Evidently, even towards the end of my five years of training, the diagnosis was serious!

Augustine baptised our second daughter in 1984. He travelled to Northampton to stay with us in the Parish of St Luke & St Francis, Duston where I served for seven years as curate. *And what is the child's name?* — "Lisa Jo, Father." — *I have never heard of such a name; she will be Elizabeth Josephine!* Perhaps, recorded in the book of life that is the name that actually stands written, but the name that was reluctantly pronounced nevertheless as the water was poured was — *Lisa Jo!*

In May 1988 Hoey was the preacher at the Anglican National Pilgrimage at Walsingham in Norfolk. He memorably invited parents, to metaphorically, *lay your babies on the altar of the Holy House.*

Hoey also continued his work abroad, leading retreats and missions in the United States. Mother Virginia Marshall, former Superior of the All Saints Sisters of the Poor reflected,

Four of the community participated in Fr Hoey's missions. He had previously given retreats at All Saints Convent. As a result of these missions there were four lifelong relationships which emerged. One was with Chuck and Joan Hux and two other of my friends.

Mother Emily Ann Lindsey, of the same community, recalls,

I was one of the sisters privileged to be a member of the Mission team that served in Danville, Illinois. Fr Hoey was truly skilled in the theatre and made sure each evening's mission service was choreographed to the detail. What fun we had playing our parts as he preached the gospel message. I am reminded of one afternoon when we had gathered in the Church for Holy Hour followed by Vespers. The evening mission involved acting out the Holy Family's flight into Egypt. After settling down in the pew to rest and to pray, I glanced over at Fr Hoey. There he was, gazing at the altar, holding the baby Jesus, completely oblivious to the fact that he was holding Him upside down!

Mother Virginia and Hoey were both born in the same year and prayed daily for each other since they met. In his most recent Christmas message, he wrote a postscript, as he always does: *I always picture us having a visit and I pray for you.*

I have notebooks filled with notes from the many retreats he gave to our Community of the All Saints Sisters of the Poor and there are many stories he used to illustrate his points. I will never forget those retreats and the friendship we all shared with him. What a wonderful priest, excellent preacher, and good friend he has been to us and to so many other souls over the years.

Perhaps because of the increasing worry concerning the ordination of women to the Anglican priesthood, there was something of a *fin de siècle* atmosphere among certain parishes and clergy of the Church of England. Another Mission, described by Kevin Robinson, captures this apparent attempt to re-live some glories of the past:

1991 was an extraordinary year. Augustine finally succeeded to rope me in as part of a missionary team for three weeks to St Mary Magdalene's C of E parish at Milfield in Sunderland. I thought my parish was rough, this place took the biscuit. Everywhere there were fierce people and fierce dogs, many on the loose, broken glass cemented onto endless brick walls, and empty flats secured with metal plates and fastened with heavy submarine doors, the type with those big screw handles. There was drugs paraphernalia, broken bottles and people being thrown out of pubs. We knocked on every door in that parish with balloons and a message from Jesus. I remember sitting in the living room of a ground floor flat with a poor, tearful and deeply respectful Hindu woman. In my cassock she welcomed me immediately as a Holy Man. As we sat together she described the complexity of life on this estate. Suddenly a sizeable young man leapt over her 6' fence and pressed his nose to the window. No sooner had he distinguished the shape of me inside but he leapt over the fence again and was gone. "Who the hell was that?" I asked, "I have no idea Father" came the reply "That is just a normal part of daily life round here!"

Into the heart of such a community Augustine launched his mission. We had a flatbed lorry with a loud hailer fixed to the roof complete with Mary, Joseph, baby Jesus and the whole Bethlehem outfit riding on the back in the middle of summer! Through the streets, behind this extraordinary spectacle we processed carrying red helium filled balloons and loud carnival music thumping from the wagon. Eventually we stopped in a supposedly green space with high rise tower blocks on all sides. People had opened their windows to see what all the commotion was. They were shouting abuse, friendly and otherwise to their neighbours and friends while the forlorn gathering of balloon carrying ecclesiastical well-wishers gathered below on the imaginary grass space. The music stopped. Everything went quiet... There was a moment of expectation and then a familiar wobbly voice emanated from the loud hailer.

Helloo...

"F--- Off!"

We've brought you something lovely!

"Bollo---!"

We've brought you Mary, Joseph and Jesus in the middle of Millfield.

Beer cans were now raining down from every side — *Release the balloons!* Cue more carnival music. Give sweets to all the kids and tracts to the grown-ups and proceed with a mystified and now much enlarged entourage all the way back to the church leading them into the very place where most have never bothered to look behind the doors, except for those occasional opportunists hoping to steal a collection box. This was mission *Augustine style*, and so it went on for three weeks with confessions, daily mass, broken hearts, wounded souls and house to house visiting.

The only time I have ever seen consternation or something even resembling panic in the face of Augustine was when the local Catholic Priest took an interest in our activity and invited us to describe something of our mission during an evening Mass at his Catholic Church nearby. It was a well-intentioned ecumenical gesture. Augustine seemed to freeze. What on earth could he say in an actual Catholic Church to actual Catholic people? The responsibility passed to the capable hands of Christopher Tuckwell. Among the six priests who participated in that mission including Christopher Tuckwell and Chris Jackson, five soon crossed the Tiber and four have now served for more than 20 years as Catholic Priests; most of the lay people became Catholics too.

The Mission Team at St Helen's, Hemsworth, 1987

In contrast to this increasingly febrile atmosphere, Hoey continued to work behind the scenes on a long-standing project, the idea of founding a centre of perpetual prayer in a London church. This had been a dream inspired by his strong attraction both to the Catholic Benedictine Tyburn Convent at Marble Arch and to the Anglican contemplative Society of the Precious Blood at Burnham.

It had always been my hope that Emmaus would develop into a centre of perpetual intercession including the help of the laity to maintain it. Emmaus has now closed. While Sacristan at Mirfield I was in regular correspondence with Fr Malcolm Johnson, Rector of St Botolph's, Aldgate and frequently visited him. We talked of trying to organise a rota of perpetual intercession in his church and he was very keen on the idea. Bishop Graham Leonard (then Bishop of London) was consulted. He was enthusiastic but thought that St Botolph's would be the wrong venue because the church was associated with too many controversial liberal 'causes' which many would find off-putting. He wanted some other central London church to be used and he consulted Eric [Simmons, the Superior] as to whether I could be made available to try to get the thing off the ground. Eric said I could not be spared from being Sacristan.

Eventually I was sent to the Royal Foundation of Saint Katharine. By this time I had begun to wonder whether the whole project was just an 'escape dream' of mine. My Director at Burnham thought not. I talked to some rectors and churchwardens of city churches who all said "how marvellous" but asked who was going to get it started. Each time I visited Tyburn and Burnham my hopes rose but the possibilities seemed to get more remote. When the 'Decade of Evangelism' was launched I thought that a centre of perpetual intercession, maintained not just by religious but also by lay people was really at the heart of all evangelism.

In summer 1991, Hoey visited Medugorje on a day coach trip from Dubrovnik where he was on holiday. The weather was suffocatingly hot and the village alive with pilgrims:

I was with two friends. We visited the church, looked around the budding pilgrimage commerce and then made our way to the foot of the very steep hill at the top of which some of the first visions were experienced. It was just after noon, the heat was daunting and the rocky path rose very steeply before us. One of the party decided to stay, while the other two of us began the laborious climb. We were soon panting and drenched in sweat. Suddenly it seemed as if my feet had wings and I 'flew' to the summit passing countless others on the way and arriving in a state of complete calm. It was some time before my exhausted companion arrived. "How did you do it?" he asked. "I saw you flying ahead of everyone." I felt bewildered and slightly embarrassed because within myself I was convinced it was my Guardian Angel who had taken hold of me and given me 'wings'.

The experience of being at the summit, surrounded by the various religious tokens which previous pilgrims had left behind, is something I cannot adequately put into words. I knew I was on holy ground where the silence and peace were tangible and the veil between this world and the 'beyond' trembling in gossamer lightness. I just KNEW the visions and messages of Our Lady were authentic. This conviction was confirmed in the evening recitation of the rosary in the parish church at 6 p.m. during which the young visionaries were hidden away somewhere in the church building having their experiences. A wave of silent awe swept over us when reality here and now seemed almost ephemeral and the true reality was in the beyond which at that moment was impinging so powerfully on us as the visionaries entered into their hidden dialogue.

After two Christmases and nearly three years, it was decided that CR would withdraw from the Royal Foundation of Saint Katharine as there were insufficient brethren to continue. Br Jonathan CR arranged a move to a new house in Burghley Street, Covent Garden and at the beginning of January, 1993 the brethren left Saint Katharine's.

Hoey moved temporarily to the Presbytery at Saint Mary's, Bourne Street, a noted central-London Anglo-Catholic shrine with significant work by Martin Travers. The street had, previously, been Graham Street and some pronounced 'Graham' to rhyme with 'Farm' as Farm Street where the famous Jesuit church stands. Hoey lived there for nine months at St Mary's Bourne Street with Fr Bill Scott, the Vicar.

However, thoughts were beginning to turn to a move of a different kind. On 11 November, 1992, by a narrow margin, the General Synod had voted in favour of the ordination of women to the priesthood in the Church of England. Many of the clergy, friends and parishes with which Hoey had been associated faced the same crisis that he did, so his arrival at Bourne Street coincided with the fact that he *was beginning to think about Rome.*

For Hoey, as with so many other Anglicans at the time, the impending debate in the General Synod of the Church of England cast a long shadow. In a letter to his Spiritual Director he wrote:

I know all the arguments for and against and I also know I cannot accept women as priests. If the vote goes in their favour I don't want to have anything to do with splinter groups, continuing churches or tolerated minorities or anything which will be like the horrific Episcopalian situation in the USA. I shall, with extreme reluctance, have to leave the Anglican Communion. This thought at my age fills me with the utmost DISMAY but I can't see any alternative. At my own ordination I told God I wanted to consecrate my life to the cause of unity. So what now..?

The moment of final decision occurred for Hoey in France while he was visiting a friend, near Albi. He visited an old, but not over-popular Marian shrine, nearby at Livron.

I visited the Shrine every day for a week because I warmed to the 'feel' of it. The question of women's ordination was very much in my mind and prayer and I realised I must make a decision and not go on dithering. When ten days had gone by it had become clear that I had to enter into communion with Peter... not any dramatic moment, just a gradual unfolding. I had said on my first visit, 'Mary, I want to know before I leave here what I ought to do about leaving the C of E. I had no particular experience, no vision. Our Lady was matter of fact, verging on demanding. I knew when I left what I had to do.

A health problem arose very soon afterwards:

I started falling down without warning and then getting up again. I fell on my head while saying mass in the Church and was taken away by ambulance — after three weeks in hospital, I emerged with a pacemaker. For convalescence I went to stay with my sister in Sherbourne.

Hoey wrote to Cardinal Hume. He had no expectations, at the age of 79, of being able to serve as a priest and many questions about how, if at all, he would be able to continue in the religious life. He received a swift reply and accepted the Cardinal's invitation to go to see him. This meeting was on the day of the Consecration of Lindsay Urwin as an Anglican Bishop in Westminster Abbey. Hoey arrived at the celebratory reception for the new Anglican Bishop but had left an empty

St Michael's Priory

reserved seat in the Abbey. The Cardinal told him to come back in a week.

St Michael's Priory, Burghley Street in Covent Garden opened on Michaelmas Day, 29 September 1993. Hoey had moved in for these festivities. Fr Eric Simmons (previously Superior) was Prior of the House, with the other brethren being Mark, Roy and Christopher. However, despite the move to the new CR house, by now the more fundamental movement towards Rome was quietly under way.

chapter 9

Catholic Life

THE EARLY 1990s were a period of uncertainty and turmoil for a significant number of Anglican clergy and laity. The General Synod of the Church of England had voted narrowly in favour of the ordination of women to the priesthood on 11 November, 1992, ten months before the opening of St Michael's Priory. For some, the announcement of the result of the vote was the moment when they knew what they had to do. For some, it was a confirmation of what their conscience had already been telling them. For some, it was a shock which began a process. Hoey had privately concluded some time before the vote that were the Church of England to ordain women to the priesthood, he would have to become a Roman Catholic. It was not a crisis but simply a moment to embark on a new phase of his spiritual journey.

At a human level, however, there were a number of consequences of this inner decision, already shared with Cardinal Hume, and many questions arose. At the moment when the exploration of Reception into Full Communion with the Catholic Church began, Hoey had no expectations of being ordained due to his age — nearly 80. He looked back on his life as a member of the Community of the Resurrection and hoped that somehow this could continue albeit that he would be in Communion with Rome not Canterbury.

Perhaps partly as a result of the high levels of personal stress being experienced, records of this period are sparse. The Catholic hierarchy seemed to be caught somewhat unawares by the growing evidence that at this moment the talk by Anglicans about "crossing the Tiber" was going to turn into a movement of some significance, especially among the clergy. Their apparent desire to play down the number of conversions means that press coverage of the years concerned was also relatively thin. Paradoxically this critical episode in Hoey's life is the one in which hard facts, dates, recollections and the sequence of events have proved the most difficult to find.

At the time, there was exploration of many possible paths to Rome for both individuals, and parish groups. The idea of a 'Personal Prelature', already provided for in The Code of Canon Law and operating for Opus Dei, fell by the wayside at an early stage, while the concept of an 'Ordinariate' as later realised by Pope Benedict XVI lay far in the future. In the mid-1990s, discussions were mainly at diocesan level and decisions mainly on an individual basis although some of the discussions and decisions reached the desk of the Prefect of the Congregation for the Doctrine of the Faith, Cardinal Joseph Ratzinger. Although many at the time regretted the seeming impossibility of groups of Anglicans being received with their priest it is not unlikely that the experience of those who 'swam the Tiber' in the 1990s informed Ratzinger's thinking to such an extent that as Pope he was able to implement a new juridical structure for Anglican converts in the Apostolic Constitution, *Anglicanorum Coetibus.*

In the absence of a special 'scheme', the Archdiocese of Westminster, under Cardinal Hume, facilitated the reception and ordination of a number of former Anglican clergy after only a relatively short period of discernment and formation.

'D-day' in the synodical and parliamentary process within the Church of England was 22 February 1994, the date of the "Promulgation of the Canon", a step which permitted the lawful ordination of women priests in the Church of England and also inaugurated the availability of financial payments to Anglican clergy who resigned from their posts — commonly referred to at the time as the 'compensation'— although this was not applicable to Hoey as he was already beyond retirement age.

Hoey returned to see the Cardinal. Despite his calm exterior, it is hard to imagine that Hoey did not experience a level of inner turmoil, or at least uncertainty not only with regard to a change in allegiance but significantly about his membership or otherwise of the Community of the Resurrection.

In Hoey's mind there remained the possibility of becoming a Catholic whilst remaining a member of CR. Some preliminary discussions took place within CR about this. Whilst to some at the time this may have seemed fanciful, this has now been effected in respect of a more recent convert, former Anglican Bishop Robert Mercer, CR who is now a Catholic Priest incardinated in the Personal Ordinariate of Our Lady of Walsingham whilst still a member of the Community.

For Hoey it was becoming a Catholic that was the imperative, compared with which all other considerations paled into relative inconsequence . Having made his Confession at Corpus Christi Church in Maiden Lane, Augustine Hoey was Received into Full Communion with the Catholic Church on 9 April 1994 in the Lady Chapel of Westminster Cathedral by Cardinal Basil Hume. For the time being at least, he continued living in CR's London House in Burghley Street.

Hoey's future in the Community was on the agenda of the General Chapter of CR in July 1994. He asked the community to consider the possibility that he would remain a member of CR, as a Roman Catholic, living in a CR House, attending the Offices and community Eucharist, but going to a Roman Catholic Mass outside. Opinions within the community were divided.

Commenting years later on the discussion, Fr Eric Simmons CR, said that the community would have been ready for Augustine to remain but Fr Silvanus Berry, the Superior, was very clear that Augustine must not remain in London as he did not want St Michael's Priory to become a CR House dealing with discontented Anglicans — he would have to go back to Mirfield. It was also thought by some that Hoey's not receiving Holy Communion at the Community Eucharist would have a disturbing effect within the London community. It seems that the Community's perception is that Augustine had said that he had to be in London, while Hoey's own recollection of his position was expressed thus: *If they let me stay, I would ask to stay at the mother house.*

Finally, Hoey decided that *it was hopeless* and that he would have to ask permission to leave the community.

The Chapter Minutes report that: 'After considerable discussion, chapter agreed that Augustine's request to be released from membership of CR be dealt with in the normal way. Between now and January General Chapter (1995), Augustine is free to seek a place of residence at the Charterhouse or elsewhere as necessary, and to take up such a place offered to him and chapter grants him leave of absence with effect from the date he has to move out of St Michael's Priory in order to secure accommodation elsewhere.'

> *The night before we left at the end of Chapter, I suppose I felt a bit sorry for myself — the last night after 50 years. I was sitting in my room, wondering what to do. Who would come to say goodbye? Nobody came. Then the one person who did come was Benedict Green CR — a kind person with whom I never saw eye to eye on anything! He brought some whisky. I went back to Burghley Street not knowing where I would go next.*

There were two issues to be dealt with: where to live and how to cope with the loss involved in having to leave the religious life. The issue of physical homelessness was resolved with reasonable speed:

I had been thinking about Charterhouse, but there was a long waiting list. The Queen Mother had kept in touch by Christmas Cards since her visit to St Katharine's and I knew her Lady-in-Waiting, Elizabeth Bassett. The Queen Mother knew my desire for Charterhouse. Clarence House rang them to say, 'We'd like you to take Fr Hoey now!' I was attracted by history and knew people who had gone there. I was into Charterhouse in days. There was no farewell at Burghley Street. They didn't know what to do.

Perhaps those in CR worried about discontented Anglicans had a point. Fr Carl Davies, then an Anglican priest, visited Hoey to discuss his own dilemma.

I actually met Fr Augustine for the first time at Walsingham. I was an Anglican deacon then and Fr Augustine was there to preach at the National Pilgrimage that weekend. We met in the Assistant's Cottage at pre-lunch drinks and ended up sitting together. The thing I remember about that meeting is that our conversation came very easily and we talked as if we had known each other some time. I think it is difficult to judge oneself the impact another has had on one's life and ministry, but I do know that Fr Augustine played an important part in my deciding when I should seek reception into full communion with the Catholic Church. I had been telling myself that I should go once I could qualify for the compensation payable under the Ordination of Women measure. This could, at one level, have seemed the wisest thing to do because of the financial security the compensation would have offered me and I am sure that I was telling myself this. Yet, I knew at another level that the quest for security was for me simply an excuse to put off to another day a decision that was going to be difficult. I naturally discussed my thoughts with Fr Augustine in the course of spiritual direction and I remember his words to this day. He said, *Why let a few thousand pounds come between you and home?* I then knew at once what I had to do and regardless of any other considerations I began the process that led to my being received into the Catholic Church.

The issue of spiritual homelessness had been on Cardinal Hume's mind. Hoey recalls that *at my second meeting with him, the Cardinal had said, "go to Cockfosters."* With insight and sensitivity, Cardinal Hume had been reflecting on the difficulties for an Anglican religious in facing the loss of his priestly ministry and also, potentially, facing separation from his community of over fifty years. The Olivetan Benedictine monastery offered a possible spiritual anchorhold.

The ties with Mirfield were formally dissolved at the General Chapter held from 29 December 1994 to 7 January 1995. The Minutes record that 'Augustine was not present during this chapter. After a discussion by chapter to assist Augustine to discern the Will of God in the matter and having submitted to the Superior a formal request for release, chapter expressed its mind in a formal vote.' So it was that Augustine was released from CR after 50 years.

Hoey made his Oblation to Abbot Vittorino Mario Aldinucci, formerly Abbot of San Miniato al Monte in the Abbey Church at Cockfosters with a small number of his friends present.

> *I was too old to go into a community as a novice. Cardinal Hume said to me, "if you make a life oblation, you'll be a religious and can wear the habit." I made my Oblation to the retired Abbot of San Miniato al Monte who had retired to Cockfosters. He was a grand man — when he died, he had three funerals. There was no suggestion of living there. They would have liked it very much. But it was far too liberal for me. There was little silence — it made Mirfield look super-monastic. I could not have gone. I felt that they were disobedient to the Cardinal, for example by giving General Absolution.*

Although Hoey had not thought Ordination to the Priesthood a possibility, Cardinal Hume had a different view:

> *I was placed in the hands of Dom Placid, the Prior at Cockfosters. Cardinal Hume said to him, "when you tell me Fr Hoey is ready for Ordination…" Two weeks later the Prior came back with the decision! I owe so much to Cardinal Hume.*

Hoey was Ordained to the Diaconate privately and two days later, was Ordained Priest on 20 February 1995. Archbishop George Stack recalls:

> I was present at the ordination of Augustine by Cardinal Basil Hume in Westminster Cathedral. At that time I was fairly early on in my time as Administrator of Westminster Cathedral. It was

obvious by the extraordinary attendance and the diverse nature of the congregation that he was a person of outstanding influence in the spiritual lives of many people. He himself confessed that his ordination as a Catholic priest was like a homecoming for him.

Hoey celebrated his first Mass as a Catholic Priest at Cockfosters on Saturday 25 February, 1995 at 1p.m. The parish bulletin of the Priory Church newsletter stated, "Apart from his 50 best friends we would like you there. Could we have a full church to welcome him and to pray with him?" There was a good congregation on the day.

Charterhouse

At Charterhouse, Hoey recalls, *I kept prayer going. Getting to Mass was difficult as going to the Mass at Saint Joseph, Bunhill Row at noon meant missing lunch, the main meal. The alternative was Saint Etheldreda, Ely Place which made me late for breakfast! They didn't like us wearing cassocks. I had to buy a jacket and trousers — and was said to look really skinny. There was no expectation to do anything for the Diocese. I concelebrated at Bunhill Row.*

On April 12, 1995, Hoey wrote to a friend:

I think often of you buried away in the country while I live here in the concrete jungle protected by the shades of those martyred monks who were ruthlessly dragged from here to Tyburn by the orders of Henry VIII and hanged, drawn and quartered. O what terrible things were and still are done in the name of the Christian Faith; religion must be one of the devil's most common weapons.

In spite of this, all is well with me. I have done a 16-day lunch-time School of Prayer at St Mary, Moorfields (the leading RC Church in the very heart of the City) during Lent and this week I am sitting daily in one of the confessionals in Westminster Cathedral. The pentitents are a multitude, shoal upon shoal, each with their own particular burden. It is always a very humbling thing to hear confessions; problem after problem whispered thro' the grille and so often no simple solution but to go on suffering. What a blessing that the suffering and death of Christ can give some meaning to anguish, despair and pain which are the common lot of humanity.

Archbishop Stack, then Administrator at the Cathedral, comments:

He certainly thought of Westminster Cathedral as a spiritual home for himself. From the earliest days he made himself available to hear confessions, a particularly important ministry in the life of the Cathedral. Patience and wisdom were two of the most common qualities people spoke to me about in his regard as a confessor and spiritual director.

On one level, life at Charterhouse was ideal because of his Anglican background and the fellowship offered by the communal living amongst the brothers. But I think he wanted a deeper fellowship. A fellowship of faith and the sacraments as well as community. It was on that basis that I invited him to come to live and work at the Cathedral. It was one of the wisest decisions of my time as Administrator. A delightful presence in the house and in the Cathedral. Delighting in everything that went on. Able to mix with anybody. Taking an interest in all things. Never complaining about the somewhat spartan conditions. And always assiduous in his duties and in the liturgy. He was a great example to young and old priests alike. A unique quality in someone so wise and experienced was the extraordinary respect in which he held everybody — including the Administrator. He took nothing for granted and was grateful for everything.

His preaching was obviously something valued by us all. It must surely have come from his missionary background. Anglican in style (if I might say), beautifully enunciated, with dramatic pauses and skilled use of oratory. I particularly remember him preaching at "The Christmas Celebration" — a huge event in the Cathedral calendar. The sermon was structured around the crib and the cross — masterful.

One of the innovations at the Cathedral during his time was the School of Prayer. Once more he was an enthusiastic guide in this new way of bringing people together to pray individually and in common. He had a great influence on the development of the School of Spirituality.

The texts of the addresses were published in 1998 as 'Leaves from the Tree of Heaven' whose early pages gave an apologetic for the book: *We do not learn to cook by reading cookery books. We do not learn to pray by reading books on prayer, but they can be a support to our practice...* Hoey, almost apologetically, explains, *Cardinal Hume placed me under obedience to write a book containing the addresses, so I had to do it.* In the Foreword, Hume wrote emphatically, "Father Hoey has had long experience as a spiritual director. He speaks with authority."

Hoey gave various retreats for priests and laity in England and also in Dublin and Tipperary. He had resumed the slimmed-down Schools of Prayer that he had developed in his later Anglican days. These proved a welcome spiritual development in the Archdiocese of Westminster and further afield. Apart from Westminster Cathedral and St Mary, Moorfields, Hoey also gave these schools at St Mary of the Angels, Bayswater; Sacred Heart, Hove; Mary Immaculate and St Gregory the Great, Barnet and St Bernadette, Hillingdon.

Hoey also returned to Sunderland. Fr Chris Jackson (by now a Catholic priest) comments:

My last picture of the man at work is from 1997 when I was Parish Priest of St Mary's in the centre of Sunderland. Augustine agreed to come for a Teaching Week — no team, no visiting, but over a week the local Catholics got to hear many of the addresses (including the famous one on our Lady) which were part of the staple fare for his missions. People came out of curiosity and came back in amazement.

Another publication, in 2000, was 'Adventure into Silence — Making a Private Retreat', a collection of guided meditations on gospel passages.

Hoey's own assessment of his period at the Clergy House concurs with those of Stack: *It was a happy place — I enjoyed being there. George Stack was the Cathedral Administrator. Fortunately, he liked me! Endless people were coming to stay — flowing through. We were well looked after by Portuguese nuns who provided our food, etc. There was plenty of alcohol.*

A moment of sadness for Hoey was the death of Cardinal Hume. *I had often seen him walking around the Cathedral, watching, looking. I suppose I was looked on as a protégé of his.* However, Hoey was surprised by a turn of events associated with the funeral rites for the late Cardinal, as he related in a letter written some time later.

When Cardinal Hume's body was brought back to Archbishop's House [June, 1999] *I was there and watched the coffin being carried up the stairs to his private chapel. My thoughts and prayers were, I hope, appropriate to the occasion. I returned to my room and waited to give time for the coffin to be arranged and the lid removed. I then returned to the chapel. The moment I gazed on his face I heard a strong **interior** voice, as if from him, saying, "You must go to Iona and pray."*

I was overwhelmed by this and could not shake it off as I knelt to pray. I lived with the words (I had no choice; they had been so clear) all through the various funeral rites of the Cardinal and every day since. When I am at home in the Clergy House (which is most of the time) I feel drawn to visit his burial place in the Cathedral to reflect on the matter.

I have visited Iona two or three times over the last twenty years without feeling any particular attraction to the island. When I heard that a Catholic House of Prayer had been established there I felt that I would like to visit it. I did this eighteen months ago. I liked what I found, but not in any 'special' kind of way. I was just glad there was a Catholic presence on the island and that the Blessed Sacrament was reserved again after so many centuries. I realised too that in the close relationships which existed between the Catholic House, the Iona Community (Presbyterian) and the Bishop's House (Episcopalian) that the island had ecumenical importance.

The 'post mortem' message from Cardinal Hume was so strong that I knew I must do something about it. I had a good deal of inner resistance. Finally I arranged to go and stay for two to three weeks in the Catholic House in February. I knew there would be no tourists, only native inhabitants and no-one else in the Catholic house except the Lady Warden, and that I would experience the winter weather at its worst! I did not tell anyone why I was going, but just said I felt the need to make a long retreat. As the time drew nearer, I felt less and less enthusiasm and when I had a very bad attack of flu over Christmas and the New Year I felt this gave me a good excuse to abandon the plan. I wrote to the Lady Warden and told her not to expect me. However, the flu cleared up and I knew I MUST go.

In the end I spent the whole of February on Iona. I felt totally at home. I was able to concentrate on prayer and to embrace the world and I left feeling I must return for a longer period. I was alone all the time except when in the company of the Lady Warden. Sundays were like being on an ecumenical roundabout — Presbyterian, Catholic and Anglican each attended each others' worship and then all met together at night for common prayer. It is rather indigestible but Catholics were only allowed to open a house on the island on the understanding that, as far as possible, they would be involved on the ecumenical scene.

I had formed the intention to spend the six months of next winter testing out the life of prayer on Iona. If all the doors to Iona open and I go for six months and it proves to be a great mistake I should hope to be able to return to the Clergy House. I expect most people will think I am quite mad to be thinking of embarking on something new at my age when I really ought to be preparing for my death!

In fact, the death of Cardinal Hume moved Hoey in a different direction:

When Cardinal Hume died I began to think, where am I going to die? I had lunch at St Peter's Residence with John Shepherd (in Anglican days Chaplain to Bishop Graham Leonard) one day. I was struck by the place and thought, this is it. I saw Mother, who was in charge, and lived in for a week as a trial.

Archbishop Stack comments on this move by Hoey:

Typical of him, when he saw that he was becoming a little fragile and realized that there were no nursing facilities at Cathedral Clergy House, he told me it was time for him to leave and move to a place where he knew he would receive the care that he would increasingly need. No rancour. No regret — just a matter of fact realisation that it was time to move on. I was delighted that we were able to agree that he would continue to come to the Cathedral on Sundays and high days and holidays, concelebrate at the High Mass, which he loved, and come to lunch. I understand that this pattern was developed after I left and he also came to stay for Holy Week and Christmas. Beautiful! I am still touched by the fact that whenever we meet he tells me he prays for me every day. I value that.

At St Peter's, Hoey found that *at first I stayed as busy as I have ever been.* Engagements outside, and a flow of penitents and spiritual directees visiting him contributed to this activity. He continued to visit friends at home and abroad.

On one of his trips, to Lourdes, Hoey survived potential sartorial disaster with typical calm and aplomb. His fellow traveller, Bernard Grill relates:

> The train was delayed and we almost missed our connection in Paris, so were rushing. The bottom of Augustine's cassock was caught in the escalator and the braid unwound. Augustine walked away as if nothing has happened. When he fell over I didn't know whether to run after his hat or to pick him up...

He joined the Order of Malta Pilgrimage to Lourdes on several occasions, giving addresses to the sick in the evenings. One of the participants, on his first experience of the Hoey speaking style, described how he and others found themselves "completely spellbound" by both the words and their delivery.

With Pope Benedict XVI

His hosts for regular visits to St Leonard's-on-Sea reflected that:

... as a guest he accepts and enjoys everything on offer. He can be found sitting in the garden doing tapestry and loves watching Coronation Street. He never gives way to the weaknesses of other older people. He is always interested in other people. At a luncheon or dinner party he is able to sense the person it would be most useful to 'get at'. Somehow he meets a need and stays in touch with that person. When you are talking to him you are the centre of his attention.

Although the Iona experiment did not happen, the idea of a new spiritual venture was always in his mind. In a letter to a friend on September 7, 2003, Hoey wrote: *There is a possibility that I may help to initiate an ecumenical house of prayer in Walsingham. Perhaps that is unrealistic? I don't know. Please keep it in your prayers.*

For several years every February for a month Hoey went to Walsingham with Bernard Grill as companion for Prayer and Silence in Reparation for disunity. *We borrow a house in the High Street and have it to ourselves. We live in silence all day. We rise at 5 a.m. We observe the full office, each part said in a different Christian space — there are two Catholic, two Anglican, 2 Orthodox and one Methodist. And Mass daily. There is one day off each week. I hear a lot. Walsingham is the Devil's favourite place. I believe God uses our offering in His way.* Grill comments, "When I arrive for the first office, Augustine is always there before me, fully dressed and sitting bolt upright and ready to go."

Intercession plays a central part. *When I pray for others, I simply pray that they may accept God's will for their life — 'Thy will be done' for them. When I pray for the lapsed, all kinds of people 'appear' — I don't know them. Who are they? What do they want? As far as I know they don't come back. Sometimes it is a fog.*

In a letter written on June 21, 2007 to an old friend, Hoey himself looked back to earlier times in CR:

Thank you for your very evocative journey down memory lane. Yes, the past was vital because it has led to the beauty and vision of the NOW. I can, of course, speak only of myself. I sometimes wonder, if Raymond Raynes were still alive, at what point he would have crossed the Tiber. It would have happened. Being the person he was, a large number of brethren would have followed him. Then CR could have survived in Communion with Rome. Perhaps I am fantasising?

A blog by the organisers of the Rosary Crusade for Reparation, in a comment on a picture stated, 'The Saturno was worn by Fr Augustine Hoey keeping his 'steady pace' at the age of 96.' However, aged 97, Hoey commented privately that he was having to slow down — he could not deal with too rapid a flow of visitors. *It is starting to unravel — it wears me out. I have to make friends with Arthritis and I go away quite a bit for peace and quiet.*

However, an event from over seventy years previously and an unfulfilled hope continued to stir Hoey: *The spiritual experience of Mary which I had in the Holy House on my first visit to Walsingham when I was told the main task of my life was to be an intercessor and the hope I have always had to be the founder of a house of intercession... so far not realised and it will need a miraculous intervention of God to happen in these latter moments of my life.* His life was, after all, not to end in gentle decline in St Peter's Residence, Vauxhall.

chapter 10

Walsingham

Aged 97, Fr Hoey, sitting in an armchair in his room at St Peter's Residence, Vauxhall strikingly commented *I would like to die in Walsingham*. 'Oremus', the Westminster Cathedral magazine carried an article less than a year later with the caption 'On 6 January, only a couple of weeks after his 98th birthday, Fr Augustine Hoey, a former Cathedral priest and great friend of Westminster Cathedral, left London and moved to Walsingham to live a life of prayer.'

During his first visit from Oxford to the newly built Holy House, when he thought Mary seemed a *live person*, Hoey had *realised that I had a vocation to be an intercessor*. Looking over his life before moving to Walsingham, he commented *Walsingham has always driven me on to the next stage. Although I have rarely spoken about it, it's all from Walsingham — MISSION*.

One aspect of Hoey's devotion to Our Lady of Walsingham is the sense of her presence. Speaking in Vauxhall he went on, *Our Lady of Walsingham is special. I have spent endless time in the Holy House. In the Slipper Chapel she is quite different but very real. The railway station Orthodox Church is a holy place, saturated in prayer — I find it more holy than the Slipper Chapel. When I hear the Angelus I often think of Walsingham. Whenever I think of Mary I nearly always think of Walsingham. And whenever I think of Walsingham I think of the Incarnation. That's why I prefer statues of Our Lady to have the Child. At Walsingham and also at Lourdes I am happy to sit for hours close to Mary.*

The second aspect is intercession. This goes back to his emergence from the Holy House on that first visit when *the words welled up within me, 'She is mothering the world.' I realised I was to share in her 'mothering' and my vocation was to spend my life giving priority to intercession.*

The third aspect is reparation. In Africa, he had been shocked by the divisions present between Christian denominations. The history of Walsingham includes the impact of the Protestant Reformation and the continuing evidence of disunity in the denominational shrines. Hoey wrote about Walsingham in a Catholic newspaper and after celebrating the joys of pilgrimage he continued:

But a certain sadness lingers over the village. At one end the Anglican Church has built a shrine and a replica of the Holy House at Nazareth. At the other end, just outside the village, the Catholic Church has restored the place where pilgrims once removed their shoes to walk bare-footed to the Shrine. So the Catholic Mary gazes across the village to the Anglican Mary and in between are the crumbling ruins of the former glory and empty site of the original Holy House.

The situation still cries aloud for penitence. The ecumenical dialogue, which is widespread and has the blessing of the Holy Father, lacks in England a spirit of reparation. There needs to be a public act of penitence and a seeking of forgiveness for all the terrible things Anglicans and Catholics have done to each other since the divisions of the Reformation. Martyrs on both sides; long years of deprivation and marginalisation for Catholics and bitter repudiation of each other. For Anglicans too, the repudiation of John Wesley, leading to another splinter group in Christendom, now known as the Methodist Church.

There is much ecumenical dialogue. Nothing will be achieved until the Christian leaders of England, with their various followers, say sorry to God and to each other for the barriers we have built. The place where this great act of penitence should take place is Walsingham. There the divisions of English Christianity are so visible.

The Chapel in Hoey's house

After several years of visiting Walsingham in February for silence and intercessory prayer, Hoey's life took a new turn. At a human level, to begin a new venture at 98 is extraordinary. Could this prolongation of his life be for a hidden purpose? Spiritually it seems natural and appropriate that the vocation to intercession and his devotion to Our Lady of Walsingham which had been bubbling quietly within his heart for over seventy five years should burst forth as unexpectedly as the spring at Walsingham.

I saw a house for sale when I was in Walsingham. I had been planning at the back of my mind but had given it up. A friend, who happened to be rich, said, "I'll buy a house for you," which he did. There were a few weeks before the buying of the house and I moved in on the Epiphany, January 6, 2014. When I've been moving on to something else I've never had any problem about doing the next thing.

Hoey's life at home in Walsingham follows the same routine as in the February month-long retreats:

0500	Rise — go to chapel in dressing gown
	Office of Readings and 30 minutes' silence
0830	Morning Prayer
0930	Mass (Church of Annunciation) or 1200 (Catholic Shrine)
	Terce in the Shrine or in the house
1500	None in Orthodox Chapel or Anglican Shrine or Catholic Shrine
1730	Evening Prayer at Anglican Shrine (from the Divine Office)
1930	Coffee and planning the next day
2000	Compline (in house)

There is one day off per week when he says Morning & Evening Prayer and attends Mass.

Of his Benedictine Oblation, Hoey says, *It has kept me faithful to a monastic timetable with the offices — the same timetable I observed at Mirfield. I don't feel any great break — I've just gone on doing the same things. After becoming a Catholic I stayed a lot at Cockfosters — for a week or two weeks at a time. I don't really miss the Mirfield Community and I don't mind living alone — I had two years' practice of it at Emmaus. But I like people.*

Hoey's sharing in Our Lady's 'mothering' of the world includes others through a group of intercessors. Bernard Grill explains that "every month he sends a group of us a list of intentions to unite us all in our daily prayers. This, I am sure, requires a good deal of thought and planning, not to mention the practicalities of typing, copying and posting."

Of his daily life, Hoey says, *The day isn't really long enough –there are all sorts of things to do. I do all the laundry and ironing — I've always liked ironing. Penitents still come from London… I have tried to get them hitched up in London but some persist. I look at the house from a monastic angle. I would welcome anyone coming to live here if they wanted to follow the rule.*

Hoey is well known to the Administrator at the Anglican Shrine of Our Lady of Walsingham until summer 2015, Rt Revd Lindsay Urwin OGS and the newly-arrived Rector of the Catholic Shrine, Mgr John Armitage. Their personal reflections bring the story up to date, weaving past and present. Bishop Urwin begins:

There are few people so memorable that you recall exactly your first encounter with them. Fr Augustine is one such! As it happens it was here in Walsingham when as a young priest I attended the February retreat for priests and he was the conductor. I cannot remember any of the addresses but I did know then, as I did when I first saw and heard Michael Ramsey preach that I was near someone who knew the Lord other than by hearsay; one who had moved way beyond the nursery slopes of the spiritual life on which I was flaying around at the time. He seemed near the edge of Glory.

He became my confessor. I don't remember asking him. I think he told me that it would be so. It continued to be so until he became a Catholic.

It's not fitting to talk too much about one's confessor, still less of the encounters in that most blessed of places, the confessional. What I will say is that I have followed a tradition he used with me. When the penitent concludes his or her confession and asks for penance, advice and absolution, the first thing I say is 'Amen', then 'Thank you'. The first time I heard Fr Augustine express his thankfulness for the opportunity of listening to my tale of woes and wounds I found it arresting and thought it strange. The longer I have been a confessor myself the more have I come to understand the sentiment.

He had a habit in those days of calling to mind the great heroes of the Anglo-Catholic movement, giving me books to read. *You must read about Fr Wainwright. Have you read the life of Mother Mirabel? Get a copy of Walsingham Way.* I think I remember him sighing quite a lot, though I doubt he noticed he was doing it. And he always encouraged devotion to Our Lady. She understands priests. I doubt he was hard enough on me, though there was never any question of the seriousness of sin, and of the challenge to suppress ones ego.

It happened that he came to preach for Holy Week in my parish in 1988. Two memories. Two rebukes. On the Monday evening when he was due to give his address I had been somewhat agitated, wondering how many people would come. When we returned to the vicarage for a cup of tea or something stronger he said, *Lindsay, you spent the whole of this evening thinking about the people who weren't there, instead of praising God for the ones who were!* Years later as an Area bishop, as parish clergy began to tell me why so many people were 'away', I would find myself telling them not to worry about how many people were away, but bless God for the ones there. I wasn't counting!

On the Wednesday of that Holy Week I had to make a dash to Brighton to meet with Bishop Eric Kemp and some others to talk about the possibility of becoming diocesan missioner in his diocese. The invitation had come out of the blue. I dreaded telling Augustine that I was going to see him and I was right in my instincts. *It's too early. You haven't been here long enough. All you've done to build up the catholic life in the parish has not had time to bed in. It might be lost.* (I had been there less than five years). *You shouldn't leave* (pause) ... *but you will!* He was right.

He loved and loves acts of piety. I remember walking with him during an ecumenical procession at Assumptiontide in the days when more travellers came for the weekend than do these days. He is a great people watcher, and there was plenty to watch, kids running about the place, Irish accents asking for rosaries and babies to be blessed, statues being carried around by strapping traveller lads, and young women tottering around in high heels dressed to the nines with their short skirts and plenty of jewellery praying the rosary. I remember his sermon at a very, very wet Anglican National Pilgrimage. Well, I actually only remember one line of it. *Parents, mothers and fathers come and lay your children on the Altar!* He was a mission preacher who called for a response, and the missions he led over so many years were designed to bring people further on in their life with Jesus. When I led a parish mission myself for the first time I modelled it on his style, though I happily admit to being a poor man's Augustine Hoey, and as time went by I had to learn to do it my way, but he sent me a postcard I think I still have, written in his spindly hand, "Prayers as you tread the boards for the first time."

Even people who mean a lot to each other can lose a bit of touch, and that happens quite a bit when people move from one Communion to another. I did know I was woven into his prayer, to use his own phrase. He is perhaps one of the few people who prays for those he says he prays for.

I saw him several times when I was bishop of Horsham, once or twice in Westminster Cathedral where I used to go to pray. One day we had a conversation in the Lady chapel where he too was praying. When he said goodbye and went to walk down the ambulatory by the side of that chapel that leads to somewhere I've never been, the sacristy I think, he turned and looked at me, standing as poised as ever in his cassock and scapular. It felt like he was beckoning me. Then he went. I didn't follow!

He wrote to me when I came here as Administrator six and a bit years ago. I still have the card. "….and so to Walsingham" it began. I won't share the insights of that brief letter but it revealed a profound understanding of what ministering here means and costs and why. It has been wonderful for me that, before he came to live here, it had been his custom to come four or five times each year to pray, and especially to pray for unity, moving from church to church. His heart for intercession was found here, and the Holy House which he knew in the earliest of its days was transforming in his life. It was his habit to attend Evening Prayer and the Rosary. He is a convert who has not forgotten the blessings of his Anglican days, though he will surely remember their frustrations.

Fr Augustine happened to be here during a February when the priests and deacons retreat was taking place, perhaps thirty years after the one I attended and where we first met. I asked him for dinner and then interviewed him about Fr Hope Patten who he knew well. He often visits his burial place by the entrance to the parish church. "What was he like?" I asked. *Ruthless!* then, *He had to be,* came the reply. Those who know his voice will be able to hear him say it. I also asked him what he thought Our Lady might be thinking about in these days. *She's weeping.* I did not ask him to elaborate.

Fr Augustine seems to be one more than most who lives with the knowledge of the cosmic battle going on between our God and the continuing forces of the Evil One, the one C.S. Lewis calls 'our father below'. He knows that the victory has been won, but he knows the cost of standing in between as we wait for the consummation of all things, and this has I think given him a wonderful ministry of intercession, and a sense of the urgent necessity for it. He is one who, like Fr Hope Patten, has a great awareness of the closeness of angels and the unseen world, so it is unsurprising that he has felt for quite a time the conviction that he must come to this 'thin' place which is also and perhaps because of it, is a place where the battle rages.

On his visits he used to nag me to find a place for him to live. There were many who questioned the wisdom of a move away from the clergy home and care he was receiving in London well in to his nineties. He had a strong conviction that he was called to live and pray and die here, and it was not to be shaken. So he waited and the opportunity arose through a benefactor. I must say I envy his capacity to draw benefactors to himself!

Now he is here. It's his place. He is a lovely surprise gift. Like Our Lady of Walsingham he will not be possessed by one Shrine or another. For us at the Anglican Shrine to welcome him each day to Evening Prayer is a tremendous blessing. To watch this fascinating man of God in his hundredth year enter the Shrine Church which he has known as long as anybody else alive clutching his office book in a Harrods bag (what else?), to see him genuflect with reverence and purpose; to spy his curé hat in the pew next to him, his smile as he quietly leaves, means far more to me than is sensible, but then Walsingham has never been about being sensible.

Those with the spiritual eyes to see, say that there are occasions when you can sense Fr Hope Patten walking along the sunken road that leads to the parish church where he first placed the restored image. He is our predecessor in years but in the life of the Church he remains a contemporary, of course, so who knows. When in due time the Lord takes Fr Augustine to his true homeland, I wonder if some pilgrim or another in years to come, with the awareness of things present yet unseen, will sense *two* men in cloaks walking that sunken road comparing notes, one in a tall biretta, and the other, just as purposeful, in his characteristic curé hat.

Monsignor John Armitage, Rector of the Catholic Shrine adds his own perspective:

> I had seen Fr Augustine from afar many times at various occasions in London. Upon my appointment to Walsingham, many people spontaneously remarked "that's where Fr Augustine Hoey lives". In the short period that I have known him, I have come to realise why the questions "how are things in Walsingham?" and "how is Augustine?" are united in the minds of so many.

These few words come at the end of a book that reflects a long and noble life; a book replete with rich reflections from the man himself and from many who know him intimately and have been inspired and supported by his long and faithful priestly ministry. My brief encounter has been with a priest of the Lord, who continues to minister to, and support, so many people.

Since my arrival in Walsingham, I have met Augustine most days. I first ran into him when I attended vespers at the Anglican shrine. Each evening he walks at a stately pace from his house in Friday Market carrying his small Harrods bag containing his breviary. His welcome when I introduced myself was warm and genuine, and he assured me of his prayers and support. And he meant it. Augustine has reflected deeply on how he might support my work through his dedicated life of intercession.

But that it not to say that he is shy to lend a practical hand! A while ago, a letter was delivered to my house from Augustine, saying that he felt he should do more, volunteering to move from the village to live at the Slipper Chapel cottage so he could pray at the Shrine and be a priestly presence. I said to him this was the first time I had ever received a job request from a 99 year old!

His witness takes so many simple yet powerful forms. One in particular comes to mind: his genuflections. This action, an outward sign of a person's faith in the real presence, is carried by many in a perfunctory manner. Not so Fr Augustine. Someone described seeing him genuflect as "going down as if he has been shot, and rising like a ship in full sail". It is not just that at 99 he can still perform this act of faith, but that the action is a powerful and inspirational testimony of a man who embodies "outward signs of inward graces".

Fr Augustine first visited Walsingham in 1933. His decision to spend his final years at the shrine not only reflects his great devotion to Our Lady, but also his profound understanding of the central message of Walsingham: 'The Word became flesh and dwelt among us.' He is a priest that has dwelt among his people all of his life. His fidelity to prayer, gracious good humour and wisdom are a powerful witness to the ultimate simplicity and depth of God's love for us. That wisdom and humour shine through strong as ever today. Reflecting on a recent local difficulty, he advised me sagely *Ah, Walsingham is the devil's playground!*

He continues to touch the hearts of so many people; his influence stretches far beyond his knowledge. His gracious presence in the village of Walsingham affects all those who behold his calm, prayerful presence.

His decision to continue his ministry in Walsingham is a shining example of Benedictine stability in the life of an Oblate. His stability is found in his priestly ministry in the midst of the people of God. This is not a calling which finds expression within the walls of a monastery, but is being lived literally in the public square, where the Word once walked among his people, and where he still does in the lives of his priests, religious and faithful people.

His is a life truly lived for others. His greatness of heart embodies the teaching of the Curé d'Ars that 'The priesthood is the Sacred Heart of Jesus'. In an address to European Bishops in 1985 St John Paul II reflected on the qualities men and women need to be servants of the Gospel:

> 'Heralds of the Gospel are needed, who are experts in humanity, who have penetrated the depths of the heart of the men and women of today, who share their joys and hopes, their anguishes and sorrows, but are the same time contemplatives, in love with God.' — St John Paul II

His long years of ministry have truly made him an "expert in humanity" and his fidelity to prayer shows a man "in love with God". This is who Fr Augustine is for those of us who have the privilege to live alongside him. He is a true "Herald of the Gospel".

chapter 11

The Story Continues

ALTHOUGH THE DATE of Hoey's birthday is December 22nd it was on 12th December 2015, ten days prior to his hundredth birthday, that his friends, family, spiritual children, and many other admirers gathered to celebrate this significant milestone.

Invitations for the event had been sent jointly by both the Anglican Shrine and the Catholic National Shrine of Our Lady of Walsingham. It will have pleased Hoey considerably, not that a celebratory event was to be organised in his honour but that the two Shrines would work together in this way, reparation for scandal of Christian disunity being one of the major themes of his work of intercession in Walsingham.

In the presence of staff and Guardians of the Anglican Shrine, the Mass was celebrated in the Chapel of Reconciliation at the Catholic Shrine by the Archbishop of Westminster, Cardinal Vincent Nichols and concelebrated by the Most Revd George Stack, Archbishop of Cardiff, the Rt Revd Alan Hopes, Bishop of East Anglia, the Rt Revd Dom Cuthbert Brogan, Abbot of Farnborough, the Revd Monsignor John Armitage, Rector of the National Shrine, the Revd Monsignor Augustine Hoey, and thirty other priest friends. Many others, Catholic and Anglican filled the pews.

In his homily, Cardinal Nichols began by quoting Archbishop Stack's account of Monsignor Hoey's time in the Westminster Cathedral Clergy House. He then continued:

> This is a most wonderful occasion and we all rejoice to be here, above all to join Fr Augustine — Mgr Hoey — in offering this Holy Mass in thanksgiving for so many blessings. All of us know how remarkable this moment truly is, and how remarkable Augustine is, too.
>
> But this is not in praise of him. It is in praise of the Lord. So I am not going to give you a longer account of his achievements and virtues other than those words of Archbishop Stack, which indeed ring so true and say so much. Anyway to reflect on a life of a hundred years would simply take too long!

We celebrate this lovely day in the midst of Advent and I thought it right to reflect on the Readings of the day, as given to us by the Church. And they are so suitable.

The first reading, taken from the Book of Ecclesiasticus, is part of the last section of the Book, a section which begins with the words, 'Let us now praise illustrious men' (44.1). Then there follows a long account of the great names of Israel's history, from Enoch, Noah and Abraham, to Joshua, Nehemiah and Simon Ben Onias who repaired the Temple and strengthened the Sanctuary.

Elijah is there, as we have heard, but as hard as I looked among the names of these illustrious men, I could not find the name Augustine!

The reading we have heard refers to the great events of Elijah's life, reflecting on them in the tradition of this Wisdom literature. In this manner, too, each of us can rightly reflect on the events of our own lives, patiently finding in them, in so many unexpected ways, the hand of God and the unfolding of God's gracious design. With and for Fr Augustine there is a rich storehouse for such

Cardinal Nichols preaching at Mass celebrating Hoey's birthday

reflection, events across this great time span, in so many different settings, yet leading him to this precious place: Walsingham.

When Fr Augustine came to talk about the possibility of moving out of the safe and loving environment of St Peter's to take up a new adventure, at the age of ninty-eight no less, there was some great clarity about his proposition, a clarity which seems often to attach itself to him, or emanate from him. Loving friends were at hand to make things possible, but there was no doubt in my mind that to come to Walsingham was written strongly in his heart just as had been the imperative to come to Rome, even though that road had been long, too. Now, I sense, the pieces are nearly all in place, just trembling on the edge of eternity!

In the Gospel passage which we have just heard, Elijah appears again, in the disciples' reflection on that marvelous moment of the Lord's Transfiguration. They want to know the meaning of the prophet's presence with Jesus, and indeed, the Lord gives them an answer.

His answer refers them back to John the Baptist and his role as the one who prepares the way for the Lord. Now, it was with John the Baptist that we started this second week of Advent, and words of last Sunday's Gospel still echo in my heart: 'Then, the word of God came to John, son of Zechariah, in the wilderness.'

How true that is! Wisdom teaches us this lesson: it is when we are in the wilderness that the word of God can come to us most clearly, powerfully, persuasively! Think of the moments of important passage in your lives. These are often the moments of wilderness. For some it will be to remember the 11th November 1992. Or a more personal wilderness of exhaustion; or a sense of being unsupported and abandoned in the never-ending demands of a parish or in personal isolation. But it is in the wilderness that the word of God comes to us. Always. Or nearly always!

It is Jesus, then, who directs the thoughts of his disciples from Elijah to John the Baptist, so that they too can recognise the treasures of the wilderness.

But before that answer is given, Jesus gives them a more important instruction. He says: 'Tell no one about the vision until the Son of Man has risen from the dead.' Think of this moment. The two disciples must have been bursting to tell everyone about what they had just seen: the glory of it, the immensity and depth of what they had glimpsed! Their eyes were opened and everything of bright promise was there before them. What a vision! What a story!

But Jesus tells them to remain silent. The implication is clear. Before they can proclaim him to be their glorious Saviour they must learn who the Messiah truly is and learn his lesson of suffering. And in order to learn this lesson they must keep quiet, live in silence. They have yet much to learn, much to see, much to take to heart. And it will be painful.

The lessons of a long life teach us this, too.

Cardinal Hume used to reflect on this vision of the transfigured Lord as the glimpse of what lay ahead given to us in order to sustain us through all the troubled reality of every day. This glimpse was to keep our eyes raised and our hearts full of courage even in the midst of confusion, disappointment and dismay. With eyes on him every journey can be made.

This, too, is something that Augustine teaches us. I think not only of his daily journey along the roads of this small village, but the far more ominous roads of his life, including moments in which he left so much in order to find so much more. The luminous promise of a life transfigured in Christ is held before us all. It is this for which we strive. It is this we wish to serve in others. Thank you, Father Augustine, for your example and encouragement on the way.

One final thought. How lovely it is that we celebrate this moment in the midst of the opening of the wonderful initiative of Pope Francis, the Jubilee Year of Mercy. Here there is so much that could be said, but let me add just this thought. Mercy is the form taken by the unending love of God as he comes to meet us in our sinfulness. Jesus is the face of this mercy of the Father. The sacrament of this mercy is Confession. That is the place, 'par excellence', of our meeting with him. There we must go, both as penitents and confessors, if we are to enter the great gift of God's mercy.

So, dear Monsignor, dear Fr Augustine, the final word of thanks to you in this reflection comes to you as both a penitent and a confessor. One is not possible without the other and we priests should never imagine that we can be good confessors without first being good penitents. This you understand. This you show to us in your ministry even today.

My brothers and sisters, let us continue with our celebration of this Holy Mass. May our prayer be heartfelt and simple: thank you Lord for this good life. May it continue happily until you call, for 'happy are those who fall asleep in love' (Ecclesiasticus 48.12). Amen.

The weeks that led up to this great celebration were also noteworthy for two other reasons.

The first is that on November 16th it was announced that the Holy Father, Pope Francis, had named Fr Hoey a Chaplain to His Holiness with the title of Monsignor. The news was communicated from Archbishop's House, Westminster, to the clergy of the Diocese and spread like wild fire. To Monsignor Hoey himself, it all came as a great surprise as he learned of the appointment in a telephone call from Cardinal Nichols' Private Secretary. Others had known in advance that there was the possibility of such an honour being bestowed and a number of priests of Westminster Diocese and beyond are understood to have asked the Cardinal to petition Rome for this recognition. This title therefore is not only recognition by Rome but in a particular way by his fellow priests. Since 2013 the number of these appointments has

Mass celebrating Hoey's birthday

been severely restricted, by Pope Francis, which can only increase the significance of it being made in this case.

Of the appointment, Hoey himself characteristically said *I really don't know what it all means.*

During the mass of thanksgiving on 12th December Cardinal Nichols presented Mgr Hoey with the official decree, in Latin, of his appointment as a Chaplain of His Holiness.

In 2010, Pope Benedict XVI made a State Visit to the United Kingdom during which the two men had met at St Peter's, Vauxhall. The photographs of the encounter, some of which hang in Hoey's study in Walsingham, demonstrate mutual tenderness. That tenderness was shown by Benedict XVI in another way in November 2015. Having been sent a copy of the first edition of the present book, the Pope Emeritus contacted the authors with a request that they deliver a personal message from him to Hoey and read it out during the 12th December birthday celebrations. As the letter from Benedict XVI pre-dates the appointment of Hoey as a Chaplain of His Holiness, it doesn't use the usual form of address, 'Monsignor.'

It is a beautiful letter and we can do no better than to reproduce it here.

From the Vatican, 9th November 2015
Feast of the Dedication of the Lateran Basilica

Dear Father Hoey,

It gives me great pleasure to address these few words to you on the joyful occasion of your hundredth birthday. I gladly add my voice to those of your many friends and family members who thank the Lord in the celebration of this jubilee.

I join you, first of all, in giving thanks to Almighty God for the many gifts of His grace you have known throughout your life. The generosity of the Lord is boundless, and the graces He has bestowed upon you have radiated through your life and ministry to touch the lives of countless others. The pilgrimage of your life is a wonderful token of God's providential care for all of us.

It is a particular joy for me to acknowledge the spiritual journey which has brought you to priestly ministry in the Catholic Church. The humble courage and deep faith which mark your life's journey are an inspiration to many and bear eloquent witness to the fact that action in favour of Christian unity is an essential aspect of ministry to God's people. For the grace of this journey, too, I join you in giving thanks to God.

Now you spend your days in quiet contemplation, dedicated to prayer and intercession. This is indeed a life hidden with Christ in God, and a new and fruitful expression of your priestly ministry. It is also a form of life you and I share, and in the companionship of spiritual friendship I promise you my prayers even as I commend myself to yours.

Entrusting you to the motherly care of Our Blessed Lady of Walsingham, and promising you a special birthday blessing, I am

Sincerely yours in Christ,

Benedictus XVI

There is much in the words of the Pope Emeritus to show his understanding of the immense value of the example of Monsignor Hoey's life, as an Anglican religious and missioner, Catholic priest, contemplative and intercessor. How much both Benedict and Hoey can teach us about the riches of a 'life hidden with Christ in God' such as they now both live, the one in the Vatican and the other in England's Nazareth.

Mgr Hoey delivering his speech

The final words in this chapter should of course go to Hoey himself. He delivered them in the form of a strong admonition to his friends and family gathered for the hundredth birthday Mass in Walsingham. Many commented that as they listened to Fr Augustine the years rolled away and they could clearly see the accomplished preacher hammering home his message and relying, as always, on the dramatic pause and rhetorical repetition, to illustrate an important point. Here were no saccharine platitudes of thanks and the recitation of endless lists of those who had made the celebration possible. For Hoey there is an imperative, a Dominical imperative, and here he saw an opportunity to rally the troops for a battle; the battle for the Unity of Christ's Church. He grasped it firmly.

Well…

First, I would like to say thank you to you all for coming here to celebrate with me my hundredth birthday.

As I look round on you all and think of the ways in which we met; so different, you represent really the story of my life because in one way or another all of you have been part of my life and we've prayed and done things together.

It is a long time since God chose Walsingham with the help of his willing Mother to create a shrine where God could be met in a particular kind of way and which was a place of healing and forgiveness.

Now, Walsingham is a place, alas, of division. Every form of Christianity, almost, makes its voice heard in this village and we may wonder so often and pray as to what we can do about it.

We speak with a divided voice; we get used to it, and of course we shouldn't; but how can we change this? What can we do about it? Because all our prayer is divided, all our prayer to Mary includes piercing her heart with division.

There is one thing we can do and must do, and we're doing it this morning, and that is to pray together. It shouldn't just be on special occasions, it should be part of the Christian life in this village that we meet together CONSTANTLY *in prayer.*

It is not just a nice idea, it is a MUST, *if Walsingham is to become the place that God wants it to be and which our Lady Mary hopes it will be.*

Take that into your heart, I said MUST. *So perhaps we should learn from praying together how to move forwards and become the place that God wants it to be and that his mother prays for it to be. It is vital in the secular, humanist world in which we live.*

It may seem in many ways almost impossible, but it is the impossible that has to be done. And God will see to that if we let him.

That's really what I wanted to say to you!

epilogue

On the Edge of Eternity

In 1915, the year of Hoey's birth, King George V was on the throne and Herbert Henry Asquith was the Liberal Prime Minister of a coalition government while that most futile of conflicts, the Great War, continued to rage. He shared the year of his birth with, among others, Norman Wisdom the comedian and singer and Stanley Matthews the footballer. The pioneering nurse, Edith Cavell (executed for treason by German firing squad) and the poet Rupert Brooke were among those who died that year.

Hoey's 100 years, celebrated in 2015, have seen 24 Prime Ministers. Queen Elizabeth II, reigning for 63 years is the 5th monarch of his life and much in the world appears to have changed. It is significant that the life which we have tried to reflect here has been played out with a sense of constancy against an ever-changing backdrop. In many ways it is the changing scenery of everyday life that has anchored Hoey to the things which are most dear to him; God, Our Lady and the Church.

Looking back over the first hundred years of this remarkable story a number of apparent contradictions stand out. The question arises: why have these contradictions marked Hoey's life?

'Sickly' as a child to the point that his schooling was affected and his life endangered, Hoey cheated death on other occasions too. Struggling on a cliff-face hanging over the sea, being bombed in the clergy house in Hackney and having the church roof fall in during a sermon, as well as being subject to periods of physical stress and other illnesses throughout his adult life, it is surprising that his life has lasted so long. Perhaps for this reason and perceiving himself always to have been on 'borrowed time', he has lived and continues to live, one day at a time.

The conversations we have been privileged to have with Hoey in preparing this book also uncovered a contradiction at the heart of his ministry as a Mirfield Father between doing the things he was good at and became famous for (Missions, Preaching and to some extent 'drama') and the inner sense which he has had for most of his adult life to withdraw from the busyness of those activities, important and valuable as they have been, to establish what he describes a 'house of

intercession'. His previous attempts to do so in the form of Emmaus
at Manchester and Sunderland and thoughts of heeding the post-
mortem call of Cardinal Hume to go to Iona did not endure. It is clear
though, that what has endured is the imperative, first experienced as
the supernatural call of Our Lady in Walsingham and confirmed in
human form by Mother Millicent Mary at Burnham Abbey that this
work of intercession and a contemplative life are what he was meant to
do. Blessed John Henry Newman, in his Meditation, wrote,

> God has created me
> to do Him some definite service.
> He has committed some work to me
> which He has not committed to another.
> I HAVE A MISSION
> I may never know it in this life
> but I shall be told it in the next.

Unlike Newman, Hoey knows what his mission in this life is; to
intercede for the needs of poor souls, the Church and the world and to
share in Mary's act of 'mothering' and through this to heal the wounds
of Christian disunity. The contradiction up to the age of 98 was that he
was needed for other work. The constant flow of penitents, schools of
prayer, missions, talks and obedience to his ecclesiastical superiors had
left this aspect of his life to some extent unfulfilled. It is true, of course,
that, despite all this busyness, wherever he has been in the world and in
whatever role, intercessory prayer has been at the heart of his ministry.
Those words *I pray for you EVERYDAY* are a source of great comfort to
very many people.

The Benedictine life, as proposed in the Rule of St Benedict, and
which Hoey embraced when he became an Oblate, is built on the three
pillars of Obedience, Stability and Conversion of Life. For a monk or
nun, Stability is at one level a promise to stay in one place, the convent,
for the rest of their life. For Oblates, living in the world, the challenge
is to foster an interior stability which might include a commitment
to family, parish life and work. Hoey's life, even in advanced age, has
been marked by frequent moves from one physical location to another,
from one country to another, even from one denomination to another.
On the face of it, this frequent movement, more akin to the life of a
Franciscan than a Benedictine, seems at odds with a spirituality rooted
in stability and yet, in Hoey's own words, *I've just gone on doing the*

same things. What a great example of stability to have lived 100 years constantly with God in fulfilment of a vocation to intercede for others.

During the course of his life, with its contradictions, Hoey has been a quiet but definite influence in the lives of thousands of people. Penitents, those who took part in his missions, schools of prayer and retreats, rich and poor, sinful and holy have been deeply, and often permanently touched by his words and his life. He has worked around the world and moved seamlessly between high society and slum parishes. Many, fifty or more years on, can still remember the exact words he used in the pulpit or in the confessional.

Perhaps the most significant contradiction of his life was lived through in the 1990s with the ordination of women to the Anglican priesthood. Shortly beforehand, there is the poignant image in Sunderland of Hoey silenced by the need to explain his Anglican Mission to the local Roman Catholic priest, and the transition of almost the whole mission team into Full Communion with the Catholic Church within a brief period. As with all the other contradictions, Hoey looked only forwards, put out into the deep and found himself soon completely at home as a Catholic Priest entering a new phase of active ministry well beyond the age when most people retire.

To try to answer that earlier question, 'why have these contradictions marked Hoey's life?' is not easy, but perhaps we can see that the early sense of Mary calling him to a life of intercession, is finally being fulfilled in the same place where he first experienced it, Walsingham. For Hoey, Walsingham is no idyllic retreat from reality. He understands all too well that where there is an abundance of good, then evil is never far away. Walsingham is *the Devil's playground* but it is Walsingham *that has driven me onto the next stage... it's all from Walsingham...!* Fr Augustine Hoey is reminding us that Walsingham is the place where Christian Unity is demonstrably not a reality and that Walsingham is the place where a great act of reparation for the disunity of the churches should take place. It is also a place where pilgrims, present with all the contradictions of their own lives, are lifted beyond them by God and Our Lady.

What will come next in this fascinating story is up to God. For now though, we can see a priest at work; at prayer, in obedience to Mary's call, spending his life *giving priority to intercession.*

ORA ET LABORA
I've just gone on doing the same things.

Index

May Procession, Sukhukuniland

Augustine Hoey in the 1940s

Holy Week Stations of the Cross — Torquay

Augustine Hoey and Alexander Cox CR oustside Emmaus, Hulme

Augustine Hoey nowadays

Augustine Hoey at the Holy House, Walsingham

Augustine Hoey at the Slipper Chapel, Walsingham

Augustine Hoey blessing the Walsingham Village Crib

Mgr Hoey during Mass celebrating his hundredth birthday

The hundredth birthday celebrations — guests gathered for Mass at the Catholic Shrine in Walsingham

The hundredth birthday celebrations — Evensong at the Anglican Shrine

Cuddesdon Theological College, 1939. Kenneth Thomas Hoey seated second from left